EAST SUSSEX YEAR ROUND WALKS

Spring, Summer, Autumn & Winter

David Weller

COUNTRYSIDE BOOKS
NEWBURY BERKSHIRE

First published 2013

COUNTRYSIDE BOOKS
3 Catherine Road
Newbury, Berkshire

To view our complete range of books, please visit us at
www.countrysidebooks.co.uk

ISBN 978 1 84674 307 8

Dedicated to the memory of
Michael Milburn,
a lifelong friend.

Photographs and maps by the author

Designed by Peter Davies, Nautilus Design
Produced through MRM Associates Ltd., Reading
Printed by Berforts Information Press

Contents

Contents

Autumn

Winter

Introduction

I am the first to admit that I am a 'fair weather' walker but this has never stopped me from enjoying walks during the 'off season'. Over the many years I have rambled through our wonderful countryside, I have always found there is much of interest the whole year round.

Spring is when new life abounds as the countryside awakens from its winter slumber, when trees unfurl their downy leaves, the flowers of the hedgerow begin to bloom and newborn lambs frolic in the meadows. Summer brings the sweet smell of honeysuckle on the breeze, skylarks singing overhead and dog roses blooming in the hedgerow. Then, as summer fades into the golden glow of autumn, all the energy gained from the sun now brings forth wonderful fruits in the hedgerow and leaves begin to fall from the trees to provide food for next year's growth, while interesting fungi shoot up from the forest floor. Although winter days are shorter, many are bright and crisp, with a stillness to the air that provides further joys, a hoar frost decorating the trees, while new vistas open up now the leaves have fallen, giving a better chance to spot a deer or two.

So, if up until now you have confined your country rambles to just the summer months, I hope this collection of walks will change your mind.

Many of the walks are suitable for any time of the year, but I have suggested a season when I personally believe they have something special to offer and for each one I have written a point of interest that may be spotted along the way. I have also suggested a place for a bite to eat near each route.

My maps are drawn to scale and contain numbers that reference to each paragraph of the walk although for a better overview of each circuit, I have recommended the relevant Explorer (1:25,000) map at the beginning of each circuit.

Please respect the countryside and don't pick any wildflowers that you see, no matter how numerous they appear.

Happy walking, all year round!

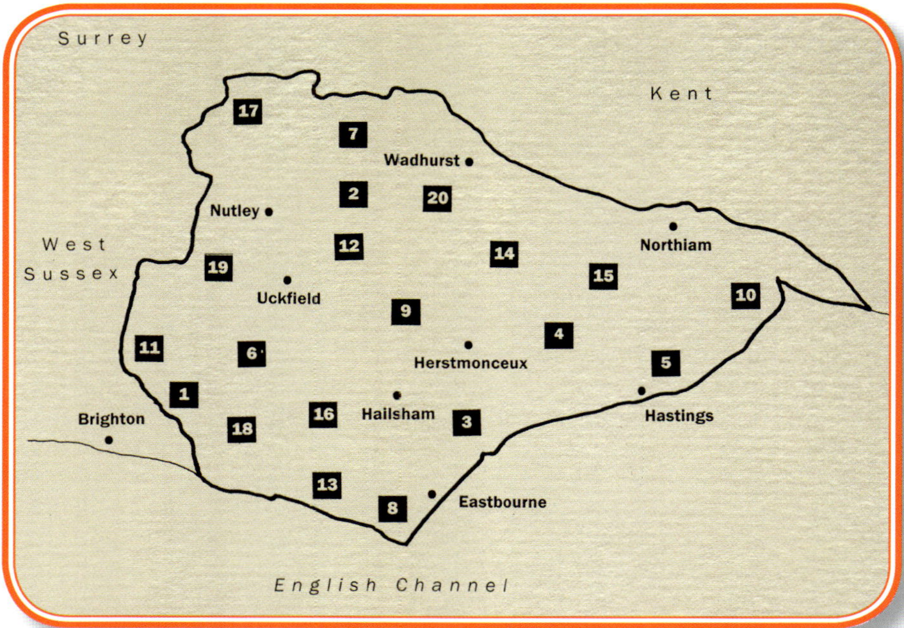

PUBLISHER'S NOTE

We hope that you obtain considerable enjoyment from this book; great care has been taken in its preparation. Although at the time of publication all routes followed public rights of way or permitted paths, diversion orders can be made and permissions withdrawn.

We cannot, of course, be held responsible for such diversion orders and any inaccuracies in the text which result from these or any other changes to the routes, nor any damage which might result from walkers trespassing on private property. We are anxious, though, that all details covering the walks are kept up to date and would therefore welcome information from readers which would be relevant to future editions.

The simple sketch maps that accompany the walks in the book are based on notes made by the author whilst checking out the routes on the ground. For the benefit of a proper map, however, we do recommend that you purchase the relevant Ordnance Survey sheet covering your walk. The Ordnance Survey maps are widely available, especially through booksellers and local newsagents

1 Woodingdean and a medieval drove road

Spring

A medieval drove road over the downs, with Brighton in the distance

With great views along its entire length, this easy to follow circuit is a must! Although a casual glance at the Ordnance Survey map of the area shows an alarming number of contour lines, this beautiful spring walk negotiates the rolling downs easily and avoids any undue gradients. After following an ancient drove road with outstanding views over Brighton to the sea, the way continues along the top of the downs where there are panoramic views to the horizon in every direction. The route later descends into sheltered Balsdean Bottom before continuing through Standean Bottom where the grassland is adorned with many species of wildflowers attended by myriads of butterflies and it is from here that the route climbs easily to the top of the downs to complete this great walk.

Spring

The Facts

Distance: 5¾ miles

Terrain: Undulating

Starting point: Car park off Falmer Road (B2123), Woodingdean (GR TQ356064).

How to get there: Woodingdean is signed off the A27 at Falmer. Follow the B2123 to the top of the downs where the car park will be found to your left, 50 yards before a left turn.

Map: OS Explorer 122 Brighton & Hove.

Refreshments: Lovely picnic spots along the route or refreshments in Brighton marina.

The Walk

1 Leave the car park via its northern (inland) perimeter to meet two tracks by steel vehicle barriers and follow the track that heads inland away from the sea. Known as **Drove Avenue**, this lovely track rises gently to the top of the downs to meet a radio mast.

2 Pass the mast and follow the well-trodden track as it soon bends rightwards. This lightly undulating track across the top of the downs is **Jugg's Road** and passes **Castle Hill Nature Reserve** along the way. Later, the track divides but soon rejoins at a pedestrian gate.

This ancient track was once used by fishermen delivering their wares on foot from the coast to Lewis. A jugg is a fish-carrying basket.

3 Go through the gate, fork right and

Jugg's Road is no more than a grassy track

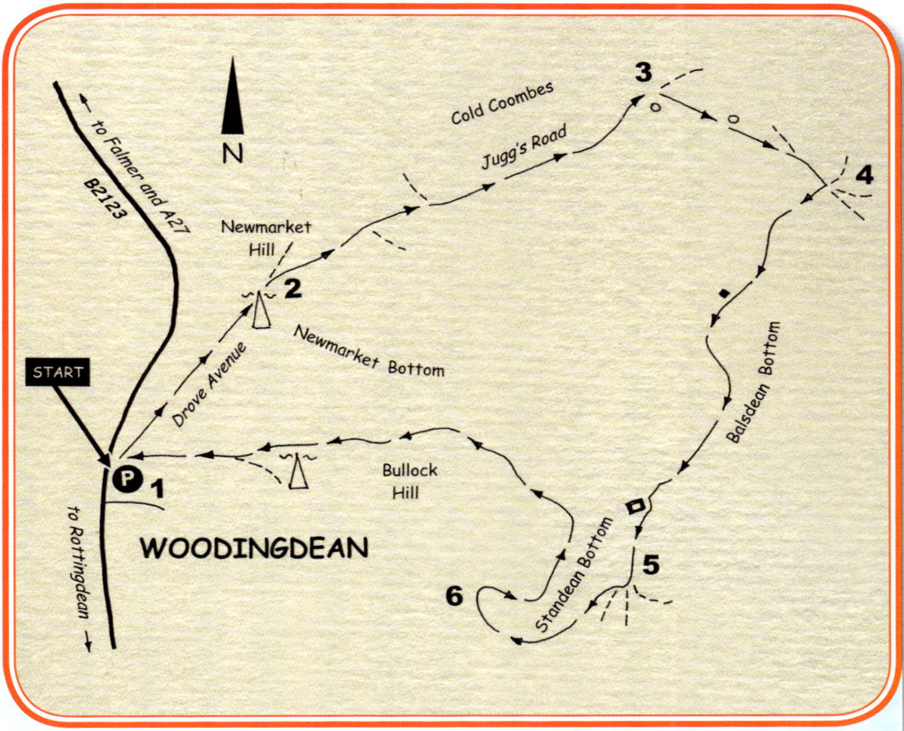
N
to Falmer and A27
B2123
START
P 1
to Rottingdean
WOODINGDEAN
Drove Avenue
Newmarket Hill
2
Newmarket Bottom
Bullock Hill
Cold Coombes
Jugg's Road
3
4
Balsdean Bottom
5
Standean Bottom
6

pass a dew pond on your right. Continue up a rise and pass a second, fenced dew pond to your left. Soon after a path joins from the left, go ahead and pass through a gate to meet a junction of tracks in 100 yards.

4 Turn right through a gate beside a cattle grid and follow a wide track that descends into **Balsdean Bottom**. When opposite a barn, go through a pedestrian gate and enter a field. Continue ahead along the valley floor and at the field end, pass through a second pedestrian gate and continue ahead to pass through a third. Press on towards farm buildings where you should then follow a cart track that passes to the left of them.

5 At a clump of trees where the track bends left, ignore it and a rising track ahead of you by turning right on a narrower path. In 35 yards ignore a path forking left by a marker post and continue along a line of trees at the foot of idyllic **Standean Bottom**.

6 After leaving the trees behind the track doubles back on itself and begins an easy climb to the top of **Bullock Hill** where you should continue ahead and pass a radio mast. When the path meets a track joining from the left, turn right along the track to rejoin the car park and complete this wonderful circuit.

What to look out for –

Chalkhill Blue

Both Balsdean and Standean Bottom were farming communities inhabited until the Second World War. The area became a training camp for Canadian troops and after the residents were moved out, the buildings were used for target practice by the artillery. None of the destruction is visible today and these beautiful valleys have reverted back to nature.

The pretty Chalkhill Blue (*Polyommatus coridon)* is in residence nowadays living on the chalkland flowers and grasses. Here, in the south of England they have two broods each year, one in the spring and the other in late summer. Their chrysalis is attractive to ants and is often dragged into their nests where the ants feed on the honeydew the larvae emits.

2 Duddleswell and Ashdown Forest

Wide tracks lead across the forest

This lovely circuit illustrates well the diversity of Ashdown Forest: from quiet woodland rides bathed in cool dappled shade to extensive sloping heathland coloured purple by heather. Beginning by Duddleswell Tea Rooms, the circuit soon makes its way southwards along a wide track through peaceful woodland before turning west and heading for the open heather-strewn slopes more associated with Ashdown Forest. The way continues along wide tracks and passes the much visited Airman's Grave on a hillside before climbing easily to reach its highest point. From here the circuit turns back towards the car park and the welcoming tea rooms beyond. Suitable for most times of the year.

The Facts

Distance: 3½ miles

Terrain: One easy rise of 220 ft, otherwise lightly undulating.

Starting point: Duddleswell car park near the Duddleswell Tea Rooms (GR TQ467279).

How to get there: Duddleswell is on the B2026, 2½ miles north of Maresfield.

Map: OS Explorer 135 Ashdown Forest.

Refreshments: Duddleswell Tea Rooms, ☎ 01825 712126.

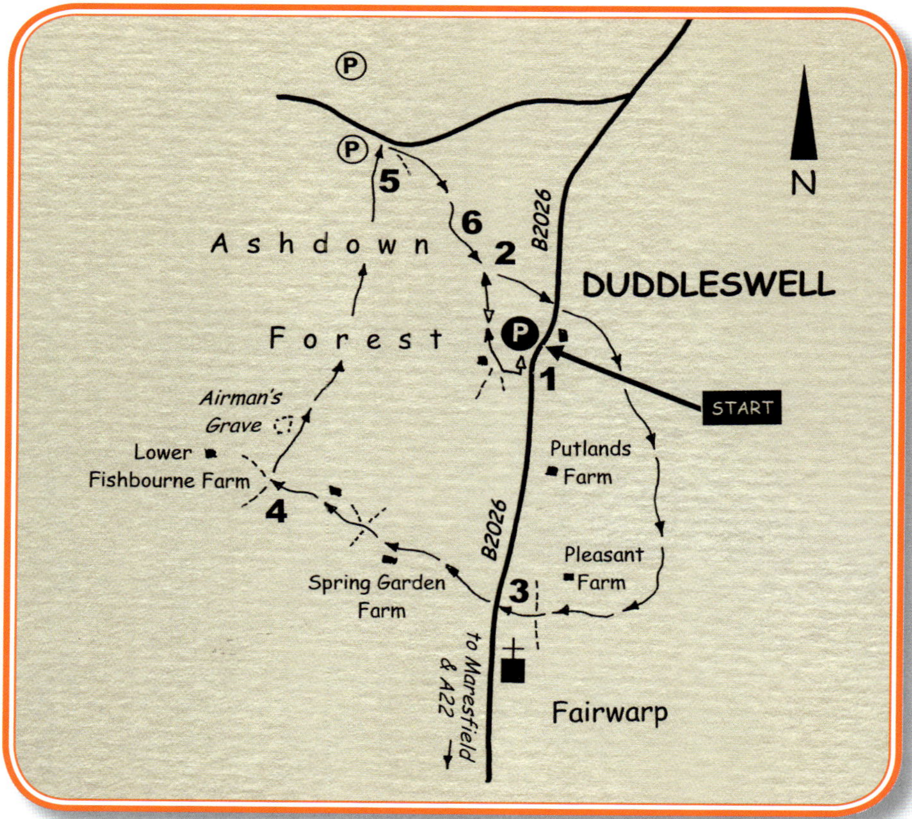

Duddleswell Tea Rooms make the perfect ending for the walk

The Walk

1 From the southern end of the car park follow a path beside the road for 25 yards to meet a driveway. Turn right, cross a cattle grid and continue along the drive until a crossing track is soon reached. Fork right here and remain on this track as it soon bends rightwards. Keep to the broad track until, with a clump of trees 40 yards ahead of you, a track is met on your right.

2 Turn right here on the uphill track that brings you to a gate with the B2026 beyond. Cross the road and go ahead along a woodland track opposite. Keep to this very pleasant track as it gradually descends through woodland and crosses a stream in the valley bottom. Continue up a short, sharp hill and, ignoring paths to left and right, keep to the track until it ends back at the B2026.

3 Cross the road and continue along a trackway leading to **Spring Garden Farm**. Keep to the rough trackway through woodland and pass the gates to the farm. Press on ahead to a junction of tracks where you should go ahead to meet a fork in 40 yards. Follow the left fork and in 25 yards ignore another left fork and keep ahead. Remain on the main track as it descends into a valley to a junction of tracks by a woodland stream.

4 Turn right here on an uphill broad track that brings you to the open area of the forest and the **Airman's Grave**. Remain on this uphill track until a car park is reached.

5 As you approach the car park, bear right and when alongside it, turn right along a very wide grassy track, ignoring a signed footpath. Keep to the track that offers magnificent panoramic views over **Ashdown Forest** and as far as the **South Downs**.

6 After going downhill and passing through a band of trees, ignore your earlier path on the left in 40 yards and keep ahead on this track. After the track bends left it meets with the rough driveway walked earlier. Turn left along it and after crossing a cattle grid, go left to rejoin the car park to complete this great short walk.

What to look out for –

The Airman's Grave

Although marked on maps as the Airman's Grave, it is not a grave but a memorial to the six crew of a Wellington bomber from 142 Squadron who lost their lives here in the early hours of 31 July 1941 during the Second World War.

They were forced to turn back from a bombing raid on Cologne with severe engine trouble and, in appalling weather conditions, the pilot tragically failed to reach the safety of an airfield and crashed. All crew members were aged in their 20s.

A public service takes place here on each Remembrance Sunday.

3 Pevensey Castle and Hankham Level

The bank of the Pevensey Haven is a good place to picnic

If it's level, easy walking you seek, then this is the circuit for you. Beginning beside Pevensey Castle, the route follows a short section of the 1066 Country Walk as it crosses fields to reach a couple of quiet lanes that bring you to the open fields of Jenkin's Green and their expansive views over Hankham Level. From here, more field paths are followed that lead to a quiet lane bordered by pretty hedgerows where the 1066 Country Walk is rejoined. After reaching its furthest point by Bridge Farm, the route returns by following the Pevensey Haven for almost two miles where its bank offers plenty of peaceful picnic spots.

Spring

The Facts

Distance: 5½ miles

Terrain: Level. Super walk during spring or summer but not suitable at other times or after prolonged rain.

Starting point: Pay and display car park beside Pevensey Castle (GR TQ647048).

How to get there: Pevensey is signed off the A27, 4 miles east of Polegate.

Map: OS Explorer 124 Hastings & Bexhill.

Refreshments: The Castle Cottage Tea Rooms, ☎ 01323 460970, or picnic beside the Pevensey Haven.

The fine view at Jenkin's Green

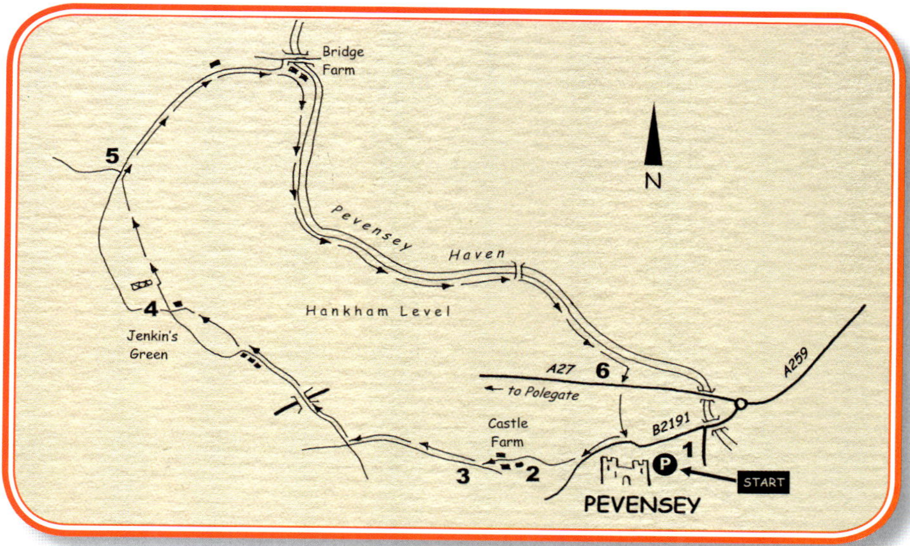

The Walk

1 From the car park, go out to the road and cross to the pavement opposite. Turn left and soon ignore a **1066 Country Walk** sign on your right. Remain on the pavement until when opposite the end of the castle perimeter wall you should turn right on a signed footpath and pass through a kissing gate. Go ahead to a fingerpost in 30 yards before turning left and soon cross a footbridge over a stream. Cross the next paddock diagonally half right and continue along an enclosed path before crossing another footbridge. Now follow the path through a third paddock and cross another footbridge and stile.

2 Go ahead to a stile just to the right of a barn at **Castle Farm** and press on alongside the building. Continue ahead between two further buildings and cross a stile. Now go diagonally left to a stile in a hedgerow beside a gate to meet a quiet road.

3 Turn right along the road until it reaches a crossroads where we leave the **1066 Country Walk**. Turn right here along **Hankham Hall Road** and soon cross the A27. After passing a house on your left named **Wood Platt**, go round a left bend and cross a stile hidden in the hedgerow on your right. Go ahead along the left field edge to meet and cross a stile. Press on ahead to the far end of the field and pass through a gate. Now go diagonally left to a stile to the left of a bungalow and go out to a road.

4 Turn immediately right along a concrete drive leading to **Hankham Organics** and when a large greenhouse is met, turn right through a gate. Go left along the field edge and continue towards a stile to the right of an electricity pylon. Keep ahead through another large field and cross two stiles in quick succession to a junction of country lanes to rejoin the **1066 Country Walk**.

5 Turn right along the quiet lane signed to **Rickney** and remain on it until it bends sharply left by **Bridge Farm**. Here continue ahead on the signed **1066 Country Walk** and a bridleway that continues through fields to soon reach the bank of the **Pevensey Haven**, the largest channel draining the **Pevensey Levels**.

6 After following the peaceful riverbank for almost 2 miles, the signed path turns right, becomes fenced and meets the A27. Cross the road with caution and continue on the path opposite that brings you back to the castle perimeter wall where a left turn along the pavement soon returns you back to the car park to bring this easy circuit to an end.

What to look out for –

Pevensey Castle

The castle has a rich history dating back to the 4th century when it was first built by the Saxons as a shore fort and surprisingly, most of their walls stand today.

Pevensey was the landing place of William the Conqueror's invading army in 1066 and, over the next century, the Normans added a square keep and formidable gatehouse. In later times, Queen Elizabeth I ordered that it be demolished, but for reasons now unknown this very fortunately did not happen.

During the Second World War, the castle was used by the Home Guard and also housed Canadian troops who carefully built disguised pillbox defences into the fabric of the walls.

4 Battle and Powdermill Wood

A fine old bulding in Battle

This wonderfully varied springtime circuit begins in Mount Street, where centuries-old houses line the way, before continuing along Battle's interesting High Street to reach the famous abbey. The route then leaves the hustle and bustle of the town behind and within yards is transformed as it follows a peaceful path utilized by the 1066 Country Walk. After leaving the long-distance route, the way turns south and passes through pretty Powdermill Wood, where bluebells bloom in springtime and the trees resound in birdsong. Continuing south on a wonderful farm drive with great views over the High Weald, the circuit rejoins the 1066 Country Walk and heads back to Battle along a quiet drive and scenic field paths.

The Facts

Distance: 4½ miles

Terrain: Undulating and suitable for most times of the year.

Starting point: Pay and display car park in Mount Street, Battle (GR TQ748161).

How to get there: Battle is 10 miles north of Hastings on the A2100. Mount Street is at the northern end of the High Street.

Map: OS Explorer 124 Hastings & Bexhill.

Refreshments: There are many refreshment places in Battle.

The Walk

1 From the car park entrance, go left to the **High Street** and turn left along it to a pedestrian crossing. Cross the road and continue towards **Battle Abbey** before passing to the right of it on a lane that leads to a car park. Go ahead through a gate on the signed **1066 Country Walk** and continue along a well-trodden path.

The 1066 Country Walk is 31 miles long and links the places and people of that famous year. It begins in Pevensey and passes through Battle before ending in Rye.

2 When open downland is reached, the **1066 Country Walk** divides by a fingerpost. Follow the right fork here over the downland to reach a gate where you should continue ahead through woodland on a well-trodden path. Pass through a second gate and in 20 yards go left over a stile.

3 Cross a field on an indistinct grassy path towards woodland ahead. Cross a stile and press on through pretty woodland on a well-trodden path. Ignore a left fork and keep ahead to pass hidden **Farthing Pond**.

4 At the end of the pond fork right, cross a small weir and soon pass a private parking area where the way divides. Ignore the right fork and press on ahead up a concrete drive and go ahead to a road.

5 Cross the road and continue on a signed public footpath along the drive of **Millers Farm**. Remain on this lovely drive that offers great views over the

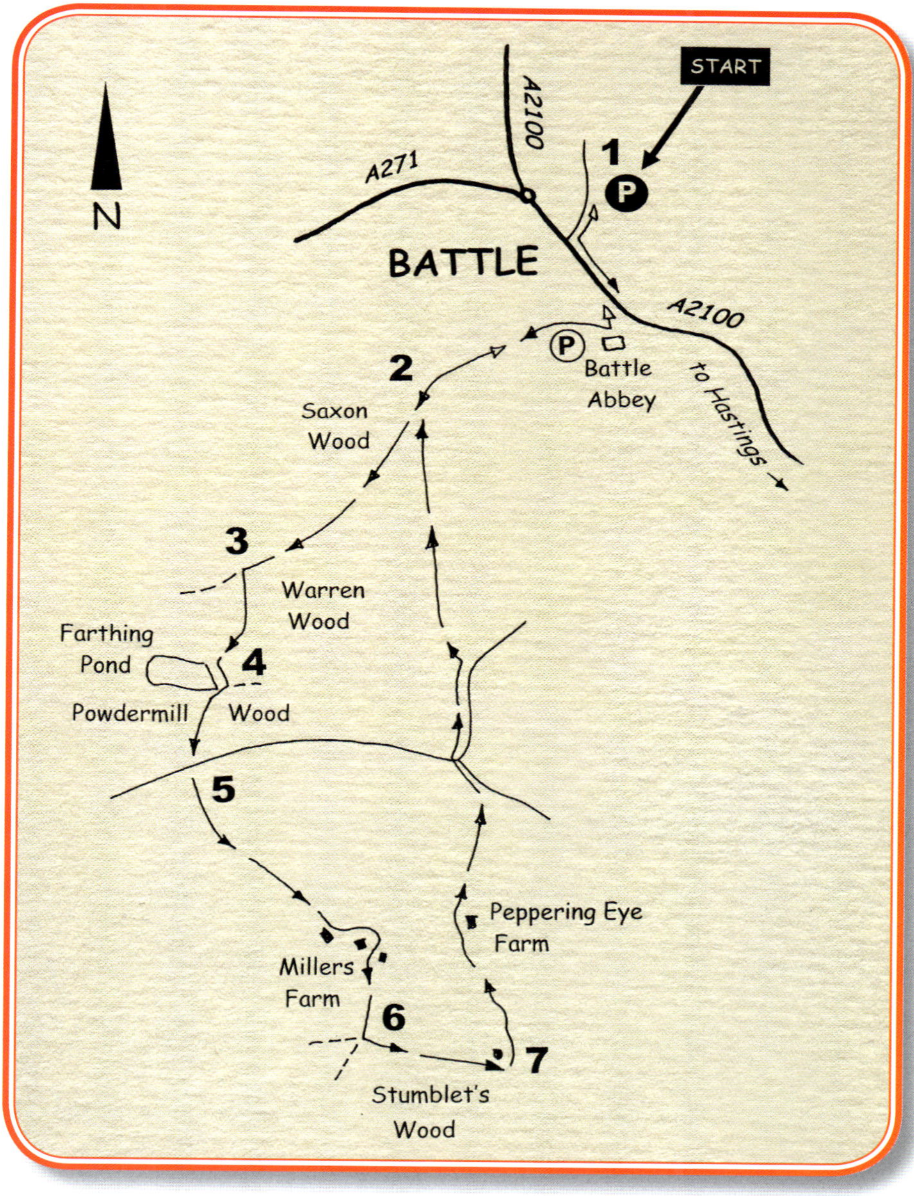

countryside and, as you pass a cottage named **Millers Oast**, follow the drive left and when it soon forks, keep to the left fork which soon turns right between barns. Press on ahead on a grassy cart track between fields.

In the bluebell wood

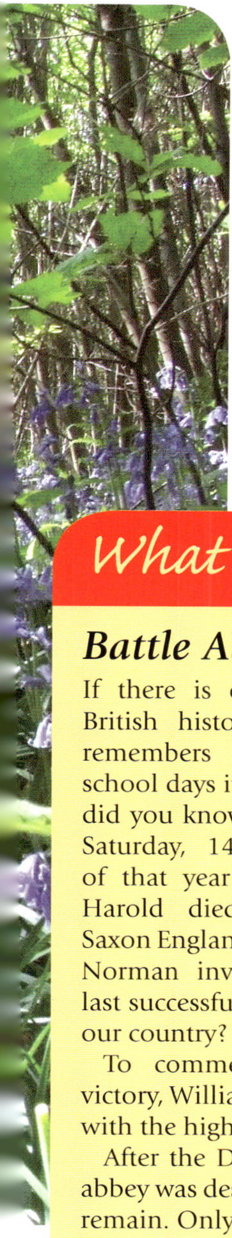

6 At the bottom of a slope with footpaths signed to right and ahead, our way follows the one signed leftwards through a gate. Press on along a grassy cart track and at a field continue ahead along its left side. Keep ahead when the field edge bends left and cross a stile in a hedgerow. Now follow a fenced path and a cart track to a private drive beside a house to rejoin the **1066 Country Walk**.

7 Turn left along the drive and at its end pass through a gate to a country lane and go left to **Powdermill Lane.** Cross the road and continue on the signed long-distance footpath. At the top of the rise, go left over a drive and follow a cart track. When open fields are reached, ignore a left fork and continue ahead on a smaller path to reach your earlier outward route, from where you should retrace your steps to reach **Battle** and the end of this good circuit.

What to look out for –

Battle Abbey

If there is one date in British history everyone remembers from their school days it's 1066. But, did you know that it was Saturday, 14th October, of that year when King Harold died defending Saxon England against the Norman invaders – the last successful invasion of our country?

To commemorate his victory, William the Conqueror built a great abbey on the site of the battle, with the high altar of its church on the spot where King Harold died.

After the Dissolution of the Monasteries by Henry VIII, much of the abbey was destroyed although buildings from the 13th and 16th centuries remain. Only the outline of the abbey church with a plaque marking the spot where Harold died can be seen today.

5 Hastings Country Park and Old Town

Spring

The Saxon Shore Way follows the cliff top

This is a walk with a difference! Beginning in lovely countryside to the east of Hastings, the circuit follows a section of the 1066 Country Walk along private drives and wide tracks that provide easy walking and bring you to East Hill with its fabulous views over Hastings and the sea. The turning point of the circuit comes when the upper station of East Cliff Railway is met, giving a chance to descend the cliff in comfort to sample the delights of Old Town and the fishing beach below. There are steps for those without a head for heights! The return route follows the Saxon Shore Way path along the coastline, where swathes of summertime wild flowers bloom.

Hastings Country Park and Old Town

The Facts

Distance: 4½ miles

Terrain: Gently undulating, other than one fairly steep descent and ascent via steps that should not trouble a person of average fitness.

Starting point: Fairlight Road Picnic Site pay and display car park (GR TQ848117).

How to get there: From the A259 at Ore, a suburb of Hastings, turn east along Fairlight Road, signed to the Country Park, to meet the car park in 1¾ miles.

Map: OS Explorer 124 Hastings and Bexhill.

Refreshments: Picnic tables are available beside the car park and eateries in Old Town.

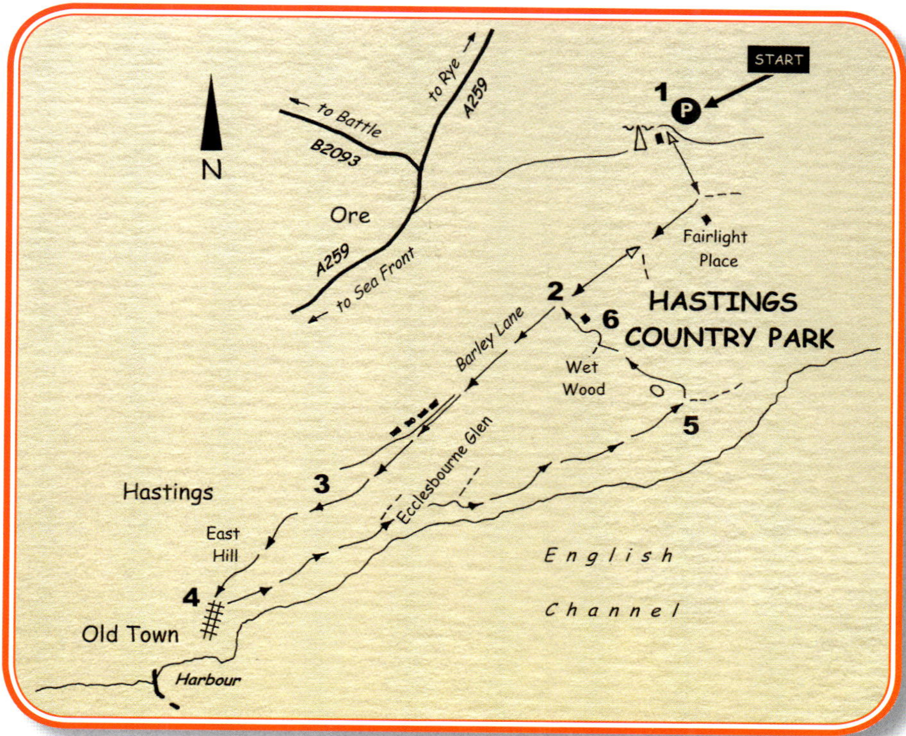

Spring

The Walk

1 Walk back to the car park height barrier, turn left over a strip of grass, cross the road and go ahead on a private drive opposite. The drive is signed as the **1066 Country Walk** and is also a section of **National Cycle Route 2** so you may meet the occasional cyclist. With a path to your left by an information board, follow the drive rightwards.

2 At a gate across the drive, go ahead on a rough track called **Barley Lane** and pass the entrances to **Shear Barn Touring Park** and **Shear Barn Holiday Park**. When passing a row of houses on your right, fork left along **Rocklands Lane**. Pass the entrance to **Rocklands Holiday Park** and go ahead to soon meet open grassland.

Hastings' fishing beach

3 Press on along the right side of this open area to reach a second open area. Here continue towards a beacon on the hilltop and **East Hill railway station** and viewpoint beyond. Although not a part of this walk, a short ride from here makes an interesting excursion.

4 From **East Hill railway station**, the return route follows the right side (opposite to that of the outward route) of two grassy areas. When the path enters trees, turn right down steps on a path signed to **Ecclesbourne Glen (Lower)** and **Fire Hills**. Ignore paths to your left and continue to the foot of the glen and up the steps on the opposite side. Keep to the well-trodden path along the cliff tops.

5 When the path divides on a downward slope, go ahead on either to reach a seat and signpost within a few yards. Turn left here on a path signed to **Barley Lane**. Go through a kissing gate, pass a pond and continue on a short boarded walkway before pressing on between fields.

6 At woodland, go ahead to a T-junction. Turn right on a pretty woodland path signed to **Fairlight Road Picnic Site** and later pass through a kissing gate beside **Fishponds Farmhouse**. Go ahead along the drive to rejoin **Barley Lane** where you should turn right and retrace your steps to rejoin the car park to complete this good walk.

What to look out for –

East Cliff Railway

Hastings' East Cliff Railway opened in 1903 and was originally powered by the water balance system, with the twin towers of upper station containing the water tanks.

During modernization in the mid 1970s the railway converted to electric power and new cars were installed. It is the steepest railway in Britain with a gradient of 78% and is open from April to October.

6 Barcombe Mills and the River Ouse

The Anchor Inn along the route

This level, picturesque field and riverside walk is a real joy on a summer's day. After following wide tracks between fields with hedgerows garlanded with wild roses, the circuit reaches its furthest point at the bank of the peaceful River Ouse. The return route hardly ever leaves the water's edge as it follows the Sussex Ouse Valley Way long-distance path through quiet pastoral scenery that lines the riverbank. Along the return leg, the way passes the splendid Anchor Inn where you can enjoy its fare at a table in the garden, an ice cream from a booth or, for the more adventurous, hire a canoe to explore the river further.

The Facts

Distance: 4½ miles

Terrain: Level field paths

Starting point: Car park in Barcombe Mills Road (GR TQ435147).

How to get there: From the A26, 3 miles north of Lewis and at the southern end of Clayhill, turn west into Barcombe Mills Road to meet the car park in ¾ mile.

Map: OS Explorer 122 Brighton & Hove

Refreshments: Along the route at the Anchor Inn, ☎ 01273 400414, or picnic at the riverside.

The Walk

1 With your back to the car park entrance, go left on a well-trodden path to a driveway. Turn right along the drive that crosses various weirs and millstreams of the **River Ouse** and pass an old toll house that still displays its prices. At a junction of tracks by houses, turn left and soon after passing a row of cottages reach **Barcombe Mills Road**.

2 Continue along the road and immediately after passing **White House** turn right on a wide track, once the bed of a railway and now known as **Anchor Lane**.

Opposite here are the old buildings of Barcombe Mills railway station, once a popular stop for anglers. It is said that as many as 1,000 tickets were sold for this stop alone on one pre-Second World War bank holiday.

Continue along this wide trackway between fields and when it ends after ¾ mile, continue ahead on a well-trodden path through trees passing a house to your right. Ignore a path on your right here and keep ahead through woodland until the path ends at a lane.

3 Turn left along the lane and, in 180 yards, turn right and follow a bridleway along a cart track known as **Blunt's Lane** that passes alongside fields. When a Second World War pillbox is met, press on ahead and soon continue on a well-trodden path beside a stream.

4 At a gate and bridge, cross over the stream on your right and enter a large field. Now go diagonally left on a grassy path to gates at the far side. Turn right along a drive and immediately after crossing the **River Ouse**, cross a stile on your right.

5 The route now follows the signed **Sussex Ouse Valley Way** path through fields alongside the scenic river. When the **Anchor Inn** is reached, cross the

The tranquil River Ouse

What to look out for –

Dog Rose

The dog rose (*Rosa canina*) is a plant of the hedgerow and is often seen climbing high over a supporting bush where it displays its pretty, bowl-shaped, pink flowers during spring and summer.

As with some other plants, it is believed to have been given the name 'dog' because it lacks perfume in comparison with cultivated varieties. The simple five-petal form of the flower has been stylized many times and was used in medieval heraldry, including those of the two rival royal houses of Lancaster and York; it still appears in civic heraldry today.

By the autumn, clusters of vitamin C-rich hips are produced that are used in rose-hip syrup.

bridge to the right bank and immediately turn left along the **Sussex Ouse Valley Way** signed path.

6 After passing a cottage, a small open area is reached with a bungalow to your right. Go ahead to pass a barn and, 10 yards later, turn left over a bridge to rejoin the left bank of the **River Ouse** where the way continues along the signed long-distance path that eventually brings you back to the weirs and millstreams and your outward path.

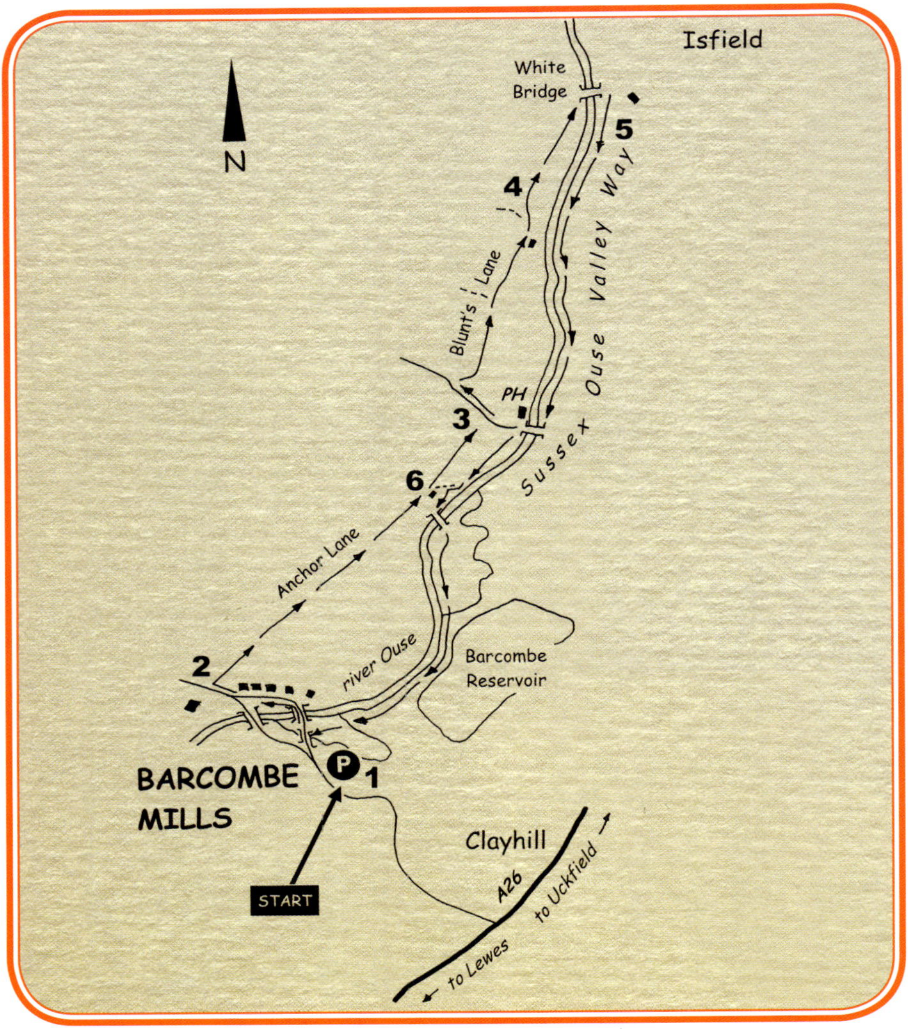

7 Hartfield, Withyham and Buckhurst Park

Passing through a pretty pasture

This stunning Wealden circuit is the longest in the book and is certainly one not to be missed! After leaving Hartfield, the home to Winnie-the-Pooh, the way follows the track bed of a defunct railway before turning and crossing fields to meet Withyham. Here the circuit joins a private driveway and passes through wonderfully scenic Buckhurst Park. The parkland is stunning and the route continues alongside woodland and over fields with panoramic views. After passing Fisher's Gate, a small community on the High Weald, the way heads back to Hartfield along a quiet drive before crossing fields with good views to complete this great circuit.

The Facts

Distance: 6¾ miles

Terrain: Undulating, with one short, sharp hill.

Starting point: Roadside parking near the village hall in High Street (B2026), Hartfield (GR TQ478358).

How to get there: Hartfield is 4 miles east of Forest Row. From Forest Row follow the B2110 to reach the village.

Map: OS Explorer 135 Ashdown Forest.

Refreshments: The walk begins near the Anchor Inn, ☎ 01892 770424.

The Wealden views are stunning

The Walk

1 From opposite the car park of the **Anchor Inn** near the village hall, enter the recreation ground and follow a signed footpath to the left of tennis courts. At the end of the ground, cross a stile and continue alongside two fields before crossing a third to meet the raised track bed of a defunct railway.

2 Turn right along the track, pass under a bridge and immediately after a second, turn left for 20 yards before turning right to soon meet the remains of **Hartfield Station**

platform before continuing along the track. Note a crossing path with field gates on either side of the track and look out for a second crossing path. Turn right here over a stile and follow a grassy path signed as the **Weald Way** through two fields to reach a road.

3 Turn left along the road to enter **Withyham** and pass the village hall. Just before the **Dorset Arms** pub, turn right on a drive through **Buckhurst Park** signed as the **High Weald Landscape Trail**. Pass a cricket pitch and later follow the drive right by a scenic lake. Some 25 yards before a gate bars the way, turn left on a track signed as the long-distance path.

4 Follow the track alongside woodland until a gate bars the way. Turn right over a stile on the signed path and climb a rise in a field towards its left edge. Ignore a stile on your left and press on between two prominent oak trees to the field end to the right of houses. Go ahead along the left side of the next field following its edge rightwards before crossing a stile on your left.

5 Enter woodland and follow a well-trodden path to meet the B2188. Go ahead along a lane opposite and remain on it until it ends by the **Half Moon Inn** and rejoins the B2188. Press on along the road, and 50 yards after passing a house named **Little Abbots**, turn right on a private drive through woodland. Keep right at a fork to a junction of drives. Go right, pass a pond and follow a fenced path signed as the **Weald Way** that skirts the grounds of a large house to reach a driveway.

6 Turn right along the drive and in 1 mile look out for a small electricity sub-station on your left. After 50 yards and some 10 yards before a driveway, cross a stile in the hedgerow on your left signed as the **High Weald Landscape Trail**. Follow a grassy path over a field and continue on a well-trodden path through woodland at the far side. At a T-junction with a farm track, turn right and follow the right-hand field edge passing **Forstal Farm**.

7 Enter a second field, fork left on the signed path and cross a stile on the far side. Press on ahead alongside a hedgerow, cross another stile and go ahead to meet a track and **St Mary the Virgin church**. Turn left here and pass the front of the **Anchor Inn** to rejoin the **High Street** to complete this lovely route.

What to look out for –

Buckhurst Park

Soon after entering the park, the route passes one of the county's prettiest cricket pitches before continuing through parkland created in the 18th century by Humphry Repton, the great landscape designer and successor to Capability Brown.

Buckhurst Park has been owned by the Sackville family ever since Herbrand de Sackville, a devotee of William the Conqueror settled here over 900 years ago. The current house (not seen from the route) dates from 1603 and had a wing added by Sir Edwin Lutyens in the early 20th century, while Gertrude Jekyll had a hand in the formal gardens.

Part of the estate contains 100 Acre Wood immortalised by A. A. Milne in *Winnie the Pooh*.

8 East Dean and the Seven Sisters

East Dean village green and the Tiger Inn

This breathtaking coastal walk begins in the pristine village of East Dean and soon reaches the chalk cliff tops of the Seven Sisters Country Park – a part of the Sussex Heritage Coast and one of the best unspoilt coastlines in Britain. With fantastic seascapes ahead, big skies above and short downland grasses underfoot, the cliff tops make the perfect picnic spot where it is well worth lingering awhile. After the route leaves the cliffs, it follows a track inland and passes through a cluster of fine houses at Crowlink to reach ancient Friston church from where an easy downhill path leads back to East Dean to complete this great circuit.

The Facts

Distance: 4 miles

Terrain: In parts, the route is fairly undulating but is well within the capability of a person of average fitness.

Starting point: Car park in East Dean (GR TQ558977).

How to get there: East Dean is off the A259, 2½ miles west of Eastbourne.

Map: OS Explorer 123 Eastbourne & Beachy Head.

Refreshments: The Tiger Inn, ☎ 01323 423209 or Hikers Rest tearoom, ☎ 01323 423733, both in East Dean.

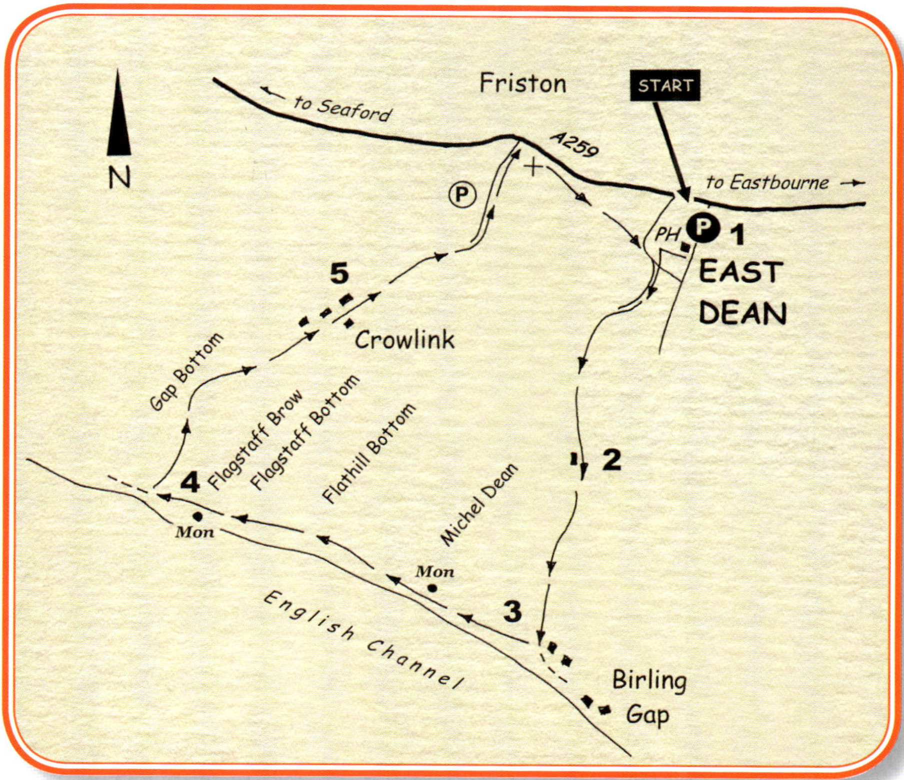

The Walk

1 From the car park, go right to the village green by the **Tiger Inn**. Turn left alongside the green to reach a road and go diagonally leftwards along **Went Way**. When the road ends beside **Underhill House**, go ahead through a gate and follow a well-trodden uphill path to eventually reach the open downs.

2 Press on and pass to the left of an isolated barn. Maintain direction and when a white-painted bungalow comes into view ahead, aim to its right and continue through a pedestrian gate. Go ahead, pass through a second gate and 20 yards after passing **Seven Sisters Cottage**, turn right on the signed **South Downs Way** path.

3 The route now continues along the top of the cliffs and it is important that you note your progress along them. Firstly, go through a steep valley and pass a monument as you climb **Michel Dean** on the other side. The way then continues through a further two valleys, **Flathill Bottom** and **Flagstaff Bottom**, to meet a second monument and a welcome seat on the top of **Flagstaff Brow**.

4 From this point, descend to the foot of the valley, turn right and, with your

Admiring the view along the Seven Sisters cliffs

back to the sea, leave the **South Downs Way** path by following a grassy track to reach a cluster of houses at **Crowlink**.

Once a smugglers' route, this track led from a sheltered cove to the manor house at Crowlink where its cellars were used for storing smuggled gin. The cove was lost to erosion many years ago. In later years Edith Nesbitt, the writer of The Railway Children *lived at Crowlink.*

5 Press on passing the houses and continue on the private road to finally reach **St Mary the Virgin church**. Turn right through the **Tapsell gate** and continue along the right side of the church. Pass through the graveyard and go ahead on a downhill grassy path through a meadow to reach a road in **East Dean**. Go ahead to rejoin the village green where you should retrace your steps back to the car park.

What to look out for –

Tapsell gate

Tapsell gates are named after the Sussex carpenter who first designed them during the early 18th century and are peculiar to Sussex.

The rare revolving design is made of oak and balances on a central iron spindle which allows it to open either way at the slightest touch and, more importantly, being less cumbersome than a five-bar gate, allows pall bearers through without breaking step – it also makes a good coffin rest. Only six examples exist today and four of those are in East Sussex.

9 Heathfield, Horam and the Cuckoo Trail

A peaceful cart track along the way

This lovely walk in the High Weald begins by following a short section of the Cuckoo Trail that leads you out of Heathfield before turning off at Sandy Cross and passing through peaceful meadows with far reaching pastoral views. Pressing on through pretty Sapperton Wood where bluebells carpet the woodland floor in springtime, the way passes the outskirts of Maynards Green before continuing through the grounds of Hidden Spring Vineyard to meet its furthest point in the village of Horam. Here the way rejoins the Cuckoo Trail and without further need for instruction, an easy stroll of just over 2 miles returns you to Heathfield.

The Facts

Distance: 5¼ miles

Terrain: Fairly level

Starting point: Cuckoo Trail car park in Station Road, Heathfield (GR TQ583213).

How to get there: Heathfield is on the A265, 8 miles east of Uckfield. Turn south from the High Street into Station Road to the car park at the bottom of the slope. There is a further short and long stay car park nearer the High Street in Station Road.

Map: OS Explorer 123 Eastbourne & Beachy Head.

Refreshments: Several cafés in Heathfield.

The Walk

1 From the car park, follow the signed **Cuckoo Trail** southwards. *(If parking in the car park nearer the High Street, make your way downhill along Station Road to meet the Cuckoo Trail car park.)*

2 After ½ mile, **Old Ghyll Road** crosses the trail and here you should turn left along the road. At its end, cross **Hailsham Road** (B2203) and continue along **Sandy Cross Lane** opposite. Soon turn right on a signed footpath along the drive of **Sandy Fields Farm**. Pass the farm gate and continue ahead on a tarmac drive. At a junction of footpaths with **Shady Acres** signed to your left, go ahead on a farm drive and pass between the buildings of **White Chimneys Farm** to a field gate.

3 Go through the gate and press on ahead through a large meadow. At the far corner, ignore a stile on your left and press on along an indistinct grassy path through the next meadow. At its end, enter another field and maintain direction ahead along a grassy path to a tree line at the field end. Cross a stile to a junction of paths in the trees.

4 Turn hard right here. Pass through a gate and follow a well-trodden path through **Sapperton Wood**, ignoring a signed footpath forking right along the way. The path ends opposite a house named **Sicklehatch**. Turn left along a drive and ignore a stile on your left.

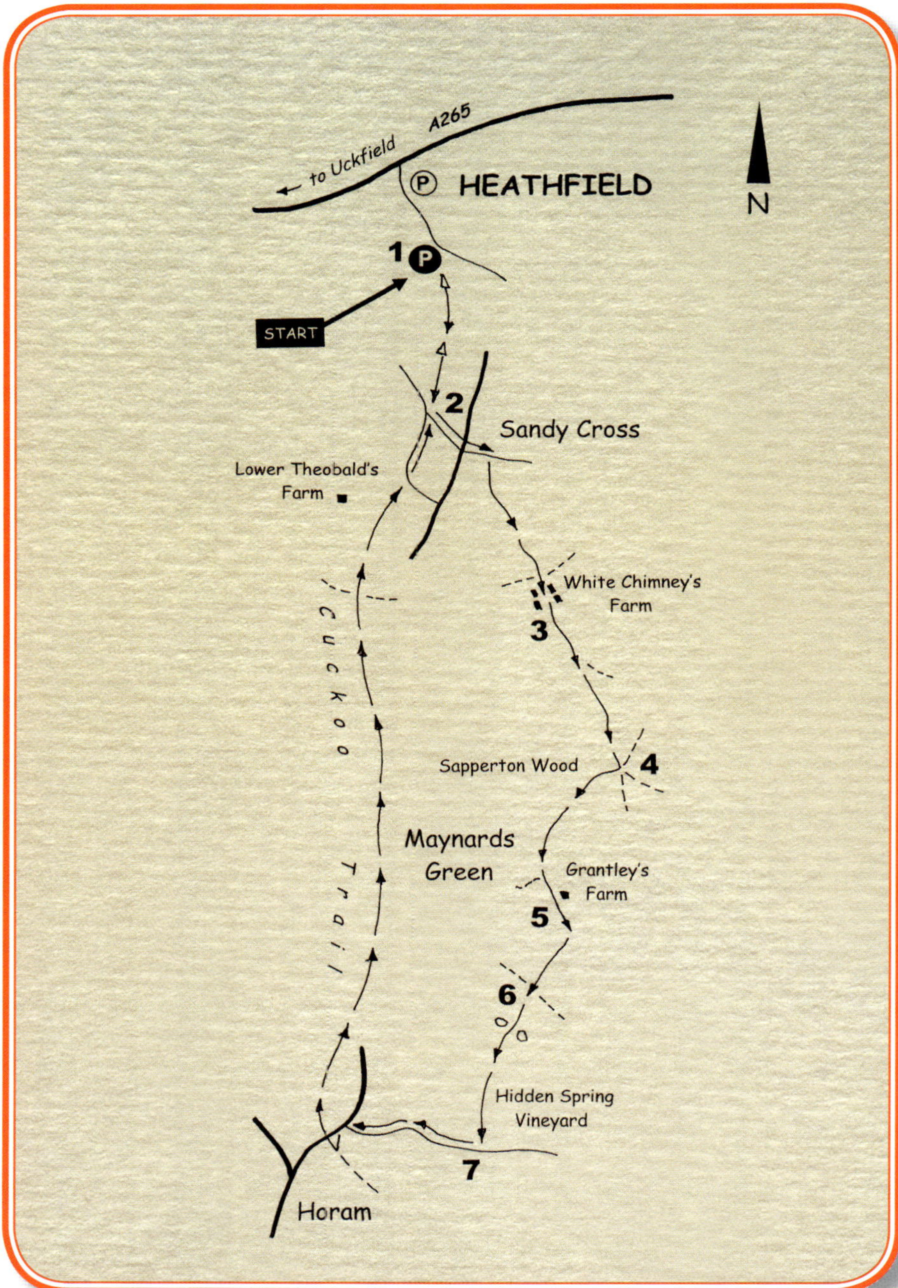

to Uckfield
A265
P
HEATHFIELD
N
1
P
START
2
Sandy Cross
Lower Theobald's Farm
White Chimney's Farm
3
Cuckoo Trail
Sapperton Wood
4
Maynards Green
Grantley's Farm
5
6
Hidden Spring Vineyard
7
Horam

5 Pass **Grantleys Farmhouse**, go through a pedestrian gate and follow a cart track for 90 yards and seek out a public footpath sign on your right. Fork left here as directed and cross a meadow to its corner. Pass through a gate. Go ahead and through a second gate where the path divides. Take the right fork and cross a stile in the trees ahead of you. Go over a second stile to enter a field and follow its right edge to meet and cross another stile.

The Cuckoo Trail offers easy walking

6 Maintain direction with a hedgerow on your left, cross a further stile and go ahead on a track between woodland pools. When the track turns left, go ahead over a stile and continue on a well-trodden path to reach the grounds of **Hidden Spring Vineyard**. Go ahead along a cart track, pass the Reception Office and when the track bends left, cross a stile and follow a fenced path to reach a residential road.

7 Turn right along the road and follow it until it ends at a T-junction. Turn left to reach a **Cuckoo Trail** sign that directs you left where, in 60 yards, the tarmac trail is met. Turn right along what was once Horam station platform, pass under a road bridge and without need for further instruction, follow the **Cuckoo Trail** back to **Heathfield** to complete this good circuit.

The Cuckoo Trail is a 14-mile footpath and cycleway that begins in Heathfield and ends on the outskirts of Eastbourne. The trail follows the disused Cuckoo Line railway that was informally named after the 'first cuckoo of spring' that was traditionally released from a basket at the Heathfield Fair each April. The line was axed during the Beeching cuts in 1968.

What to look out for –

Five Spot Burnet moth

The Five Spot Burnet moths (*Zygaena trifolii*) are one of the most common daytime flying moths in Britain and can be seen during hot, sunny, summer days. Their favoured food plants include scabious, clover and knapweed which grow beside hedgerows and field margins.

The dark metallic green colouring and five vivid red spots on their forewings make them easy to identify; the colouring is a warning to predators because their bodies contain cyanide ingested from their food.

The moths' short life-cycle ends after mating and the female has laid her eggs which within days hatch into tiny caterpillars. During autumn they hibernate within their food plants and by the next spring emerge fully grown, spin cocoons and pupate to emerge as adult moths in June and July.

10 Rye Harbour and Nature Reserve

On the way to the sea

This superb, level and interesting circuit begins in Rye harbour, a village situated on the extensive shingle beaches deposited over the past millennia that have left the medieval Cinque Port of Rye two miles inland. The way begins by following a track alongside the internationally-recognized nature reserve that is a mosaic of shingle, reed beds and salt marsh which is at its prettiest in summer. Arriving at the seashore, the route turns west and continues along another track or, dependant on the tide, along the beach to meet its furthest point on the outskirts of Winchelsea. The return route is through the nature reserve that is home to more than 150 rare or endangered species.

The Facts

Distance: 5 miles

Terrain: Level and suitable for all times of the year, even after heavy rain.

Starting point: Car park at Rye Harbour (GR TQ942189).

How to get there: Rye Harbour is signed off the A259 Winchelsea road, west of Rye.

Map: OS Explorer 125 Romney Marsh, Rye and Winchelsea.

Refreshments: There are pubs and tea rooms in the village or picnic on the beach.

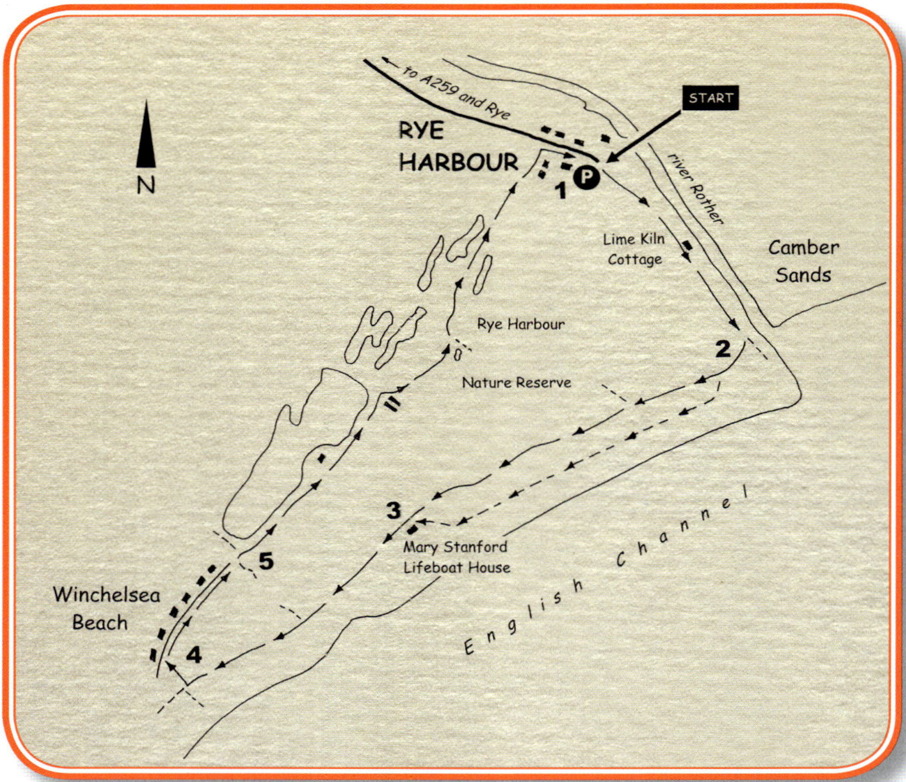

The track through the nature reserve

The Walk

1 From the car park entrance, pass the entrance to **Frenchman's Beach Holiday Park** and fork right along a hard surfaced track. Along the way pass **Lime Kiln Cottage Information Centre** and press on until a tarmac track is reached on your right as you near the sea.

2 Turn right along this track that in summer is bordered by groups of yellow horned poppy, red valerian and more viper's bugloss than I've ever seen. The way follows this track for 2 miles but if you wish, and the tide is right, you may prefer to cross the shingle bank on your left and follow the seashore.

3 Along the way pass the forlorn **Mary Stanford Lifeboat House** on the

shingle bank. If you have been following the seashore, make your way to this building and rejoin the tarmac path beyond.

It was from this old lifeboat house in the early hours of 15th November 1928 that a dreadful disaster began. After receiving an SOS call from a steamer during heavy seas off Dungeness, seventeen volunteer lifeboat men rushed here and dragged the Mary Stanford *lifeboat down the beach and into the crashing waves where they set sail and rowed into the foaming cauldron. Later, the steamer sent a radio message stating that their crew were safe but sadly the lifeboat men failed to see the recall signal and all were tragically lost to the waves.*

4 Ignore the occasional path on your right along the way and continue on the tarmac track to reach some steps with a steel handrail on your left. Turn right here and pass between meadows to a private shingle road. Turn right along this road passing a diverse collection of seaside homes to a junction of tracks.

5 Go ahead here bearing slightly right and now follow a wide shingle track through the nature reserve until it finally ends after 1½ miles at a road in **Rye harbour** where a right turn soon returns you to the car park to complete this easy walk.

What to look out for –

Vipers Bugloss

Vipers Bugloss (*Echium vulgare*) is a handsome warmth-loving plant that grows up to 3 ft high during its short flowering season. The flowers first emerge red and later change through purple to blue. The word 'viper' refers to the old use of the plant in herb medicine as a treatment for a viper's (adder) bite while 'bugloss' refers to the shape of the leaf which in Greek means 'ox-tongue'. For centuries it was used in the treatment of chest and skin conditions although it has now fallen out of favour with modern-day herbalists.

11 Ditchling, Streat & Westmeston

A colourful path near Westmeston

This gentle stroll through charming countryside below the northern flank of the South Downs is lovely at any time of the year but is especially colourful during autumn. Within minutes of leaving Ditchling, the way follows level paths and farm tracks, with extensive views. After reaching the first turning point at Streat's pretty church, the route heads south as it strikes out over fields on well-signed paths and passes the outskirts of Westmeston. Turning back towards Ditchling the way crosses fields by Westmeston Place before passing through woodland and retracing the first few minutes of the route to end back at the car park.

Autumn

The Facts

Distance: 4½ miles

Terrain: Level

Starting point: Car park in Lewis Road (B2116) at the centre of Ditchling (GR TQ326152).

How to get there: Ditchling is 2½ miles east of Hassocks, at the crossroads of the B2116 and B2112.

Map: OS Explorer 122 Brighton & Hove

Refreshments: The Bull pub opposite the car park, ☎ 01273 843147.

The Walk

1 From the car park entrance turn right along the road and soon fork left on a small lane called **Fieldway**. At its end, go ahead on a footpath to meet a quiet road. Go ahead on **Farm Lane** opposite and, at its end, press on along the side of a recreation ground. At an open area, go ahead and cross a footbridge over a brook. Maintain your direction through another open area before entering woodland on a well-trodden path that ends at a road.

2 Cross the road and go ahead on a drive beside the gates of a house. Remain on the drive that offers easy walking with panoramic views until it ends after ¾ mile at a T-junction, with a bridleway beside **Hayleigh Farm**. Turn left and when opposite the farmhouse, turn right along a track to reach **Streat church**.

❸ Turn right on a signed path through the graveyard to enter a field. Go diagonally right across the field aiming to the right of a solitary oak tree and cross a stile beyond it. Keep ahead and pass through a kissing gate in a hedgerow opposite. Press on for 30 yards to meet a cart track and turn right along it. As the track loops leftwards, follow a grassy path forking right and after crossing a stile, continue on a fenced path leftwards between fields to reach a wide bridleway.

By now you will have encountered the stiles made by the Monday Group, a band of stalwarts formed 50 years ago. Their aim is to keep local footpaths open and their forte is building oak stiles. After starting with design number 1, today's design number 18 is a ladder stile incorporating a dog gate and a lifting top bar that makes crossing easier for young and old. Their efforts must be applauded.

Streat church marks the turning point of the walk

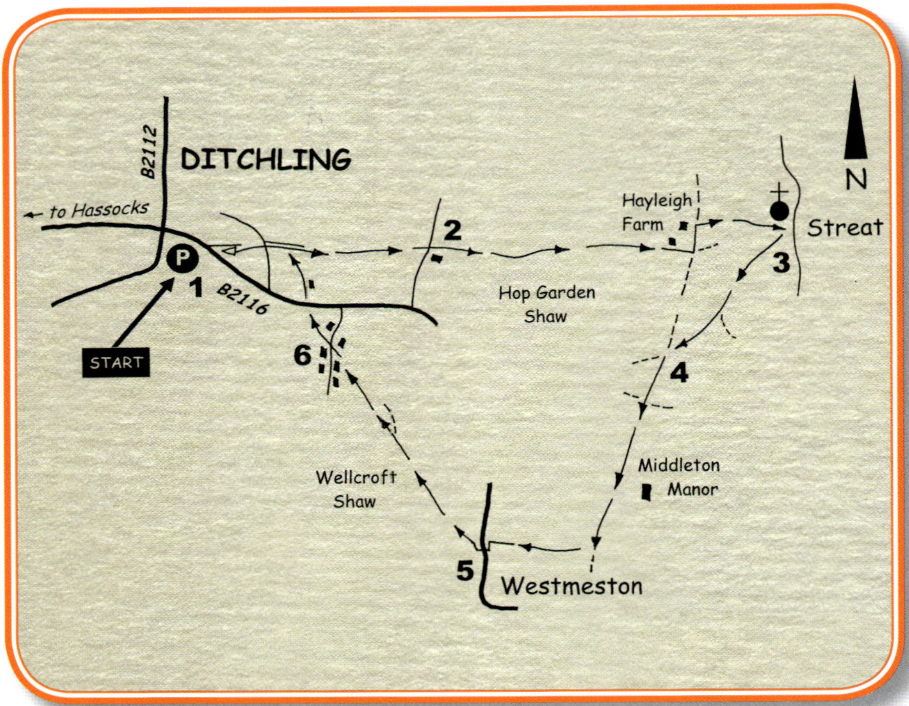

❹ Turn left along the bridleway and go over a crossing bridleway. After passing the grounds of **Middleton Manor**, turn right on a signed footpath 30 yards before a field gate across the bridleway. Climb a low bank and go ahead through the centre of a meadow. Press on through the next meadow and as this ends, ignore a stile on your left but cross another ahead of you with a barn beyond. Pass to the right of the barn and follow the path to reach a road.

❺ Turn left along the road and 5 yards after passing the entrance to **April Cottage** turn right up a bank to a marker post. Turn right here and cross the cottage's driveway via steps to enter a field. Now follow a well-signed grassy path for ½ mile through meadows to enter woodland. Bear right and keep to the well-trodden path bearing left at a fork to finally pass between houses to meet a private road.

❻ Go diagonally right and continue on a path beside **Odd Acre** to reach **Lewis Road**. Cross to the recreation ground opposite and follow a path to the left of the pavilion and after passing tennis courts the outward route is met. Now turn left and retrace your steps back to the car park to end this fascinating circuit.

What to look out for –

Black Bryony

Draping themselves over the hedgerows like extravagant necklaces, the strings of bright red berries of Black Bryony (*Tamus communis*) display themselves admirably during autumn, although their insignificant pale yellow flowers are easily missed earlier in the year.

Black Bryony is no relation to White Bryony but is a member of the yam family. Named after the colour of its underground tuber, the plant throws up slender smooth stems that entwine clockwise around supporting plants and has heart-shaped shiny green leaves that by autumn fall and expose the highly poisonous fruit.

It was Black Bryony's poisonous qualities that led to the tuber being used as an emetic during the Middle Ages and brought forth its old name, 'snakeberry'.

12 Around Fairwarp & Cackle Street

The southern tip of Ashdown Forest

This charming and varied walk is good for any time of the year but even better when coloured by the hues of autumn. The circuit passes through the quieter southern reaches of Ashdown Forest that offer a contrast with its popular open spaces. The route begins on the outskirts of Fairwarp, an area once known for the charcoal that supplied the early iron foundries nearby. After following the top of a ridge with superb views over the forest, the way descends and passes Boringwheel Mill Farm in Cackle Street. The farm, as its name implies, was where early cannons had their centres bored. After continuing along field paths and quiet country lanes, the circuit passes through Fairwarp village before heading back to the car park to complete this lovely walk.

The Facts

Distance: 4¼ miles

Terrain: Gently undulating

Starting point: Shepherds car park, Ashdown Forest (GR TQ466272).

How to get there: The car park is on the B2026, ¼ mile north of Christ Church, Fairwarp. The B2026 is off the A22, 1 mile north of Maresfield.

Map: OS Explorer 135 Ashdown Forest

Refreshments: The Foresters pub in Fairwarp village, ☎ 01825 712808.

Autumn

The Walk

1 Leave the car park via a well-trodden curving path that skirts an open area. At a wide crossing track, turn right to soon meet the B2026. Cross to the track opposite signed to **Spring Garden Farm**, go over a cattle grid and ignore a footpath on your right. Go ahead on the track soon ignoring a crossing track.

2 After passing the gate to **Spring Garden Farm**, continue ahead on the track to a small open area with a barn on your left. Keep ahead and in 50 yards ignore a right fork. Press on to a second open area and fork left on a track that follows the top of a ridge with magnificent views of the open forest on your right.

3 After descending from the ridge, the track enters woodland and meets a stile by a gate. Continue ahead and pass the buildings of **Boringwheel Mill Farm** to reach a country lane. Turn left along the lane and at the garden end of the second house on your right, turn right on a fenced path to cross a stile and enter a field.

4 Turn left along the field edge and at its corner follow its boundary rightwards and go over a stile at its end. Go ahead passing the end of a woodland pool and walk through a gate ahead of you. Press on along a well-trodden path through a coppice to a country lane.

5 Turn right along the lane for 15 yards before going left on a signed footpath and passing **Kate's Cottage** to reach a field. Press on ahead along its right-hand side and at its end enter woodland. Keep to the path ignoring others to left and right. The path later bends right around a deep depression to a directional post. Turn left here on a fenced path to rejoin the B2026.

A wide path through the forest

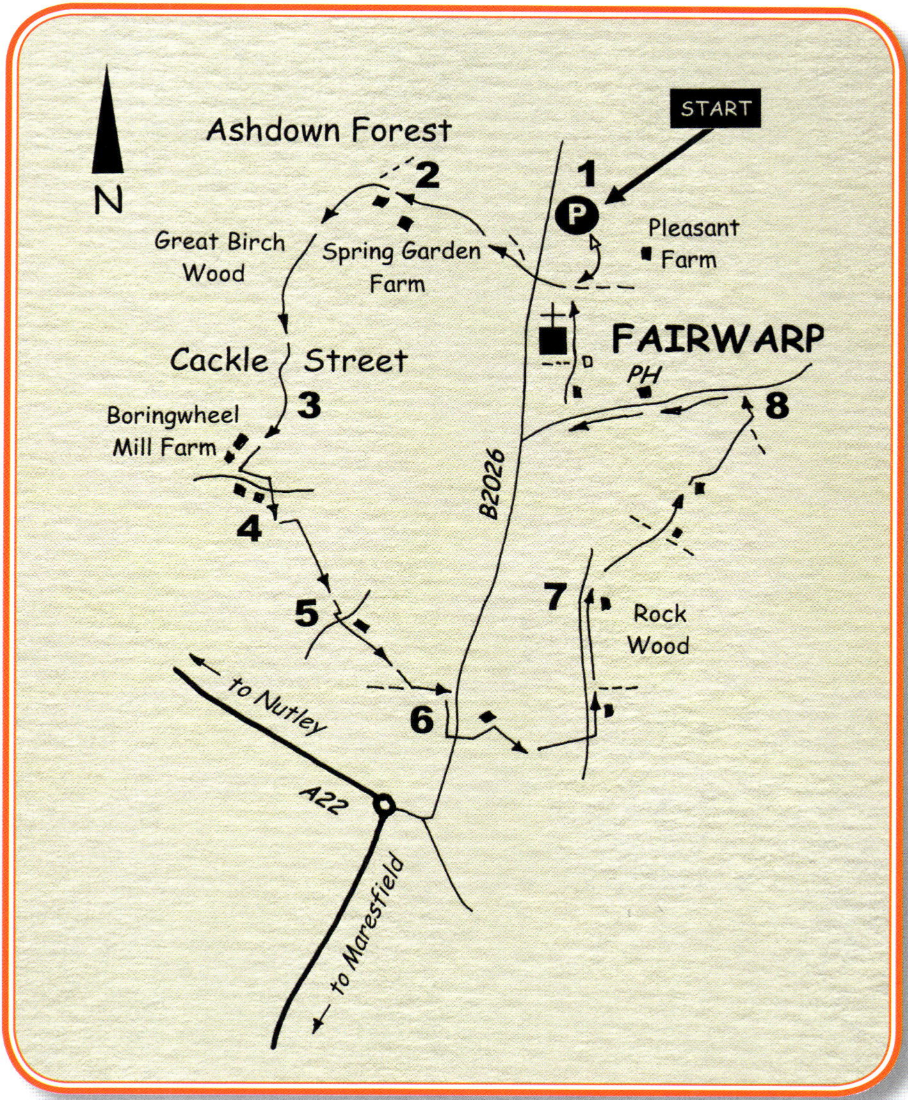

6 Turn right alongside the road for 130 yards before turning left on a signed footpath along the drive of **Lampool Edge**. At gates, continue on a fenced path to meet a field. Cross a stile and follow its right-hand edge to **Nursery Lane**. Turn left along the lane and ignore a footpath on your right after passing **Woodland Cottage**.

7 After passing **Red Tiles** and rounding a bend, fork right on a signed woodland path that meets a wide track. Turn right along the track and at a fork, keep left and press on to a drive by **Summerford Farm**. Go ahead and when the drive ends at the gate to **Arnold's**, continue ahead on a wide grassy path that soon narrows. Keep to the path as it bends right and at a T-junction with a broad track, go left along the track. When a path enters from the right by a gate, go ahead but fork left in 20 yards to the village street at **Fairwarp**.

8 Turn left along the road, pass the **Foresters pub** and 35 yards after passing the village green, turn right on a track by **Spinners** and **Spinners Cottage**. At a right bend with tennis courts on your right, ignore a path to the left but in 10 yards fork left on a woodland path that passes the rear of **Christ church**. Keep to the path and later go over a crossing track to retrace your earlier steps to return to the car park.

What to look out for –

Blackthorn

Blackthorn (*Prunus spinosa*) grows along parts of this route and is particularly abundant at point 4. The pure white flowers appear in March and the fruit, called a sloe, is ripe from September to November.

The sloe resembles a small plum and is blue-black in colour with an attractive bloom but, unlike the plum, it is highly astringent and inedible, although it does make sloe gin. With patience being the main ingredient, the recipe is simple: *320g of sloes with skins well pricked, 160g of caster sugar and 70cl of cheap gin.* Mix equal quantities of each divided in two bottles and shake daily for one week then weekly for two months before straining out the sloes. The resulting red liqueur will be ready to enjoy by Christmas.

13 Exceat, Friston Forest & Litlington

In the forest

This stunning energetic route is superb at any time of the year but the autumn colours add to what is already a not-to-be-missed walk. Beginning at Exceat, the way soon passes through the picturesque village of Westdean which, together with Exceat, were important villages during the 1400s, raising more taxes for the king's coffers than nearby Lewes. Both villages suffered the ravages of the Black Death and occasional French raids and today only Westdean remains. Exceat was abandoned during the mid 1450s. After walking wide tracks through the tranquillity of Friston Forest, the way descends into the Cuckmere Valley to the pretty village of Litlington from where the route returns to Exceat via Westdean.

Distance: 5½ miles

Terrain: Hilly but well within the capability of a person of average fitness.

Starting point: Seven Sisters Country Park pay and display car park (GR TQ518995).

How to get there: The car park is off the A259 at Exceat, halfway between Eastbourne and Seaford.

Map: OS Explorer 123 Eastbourne & Beachy Head

Refreshments: The Plough & Harrow pub, Litlington, ☎ 01323 870623

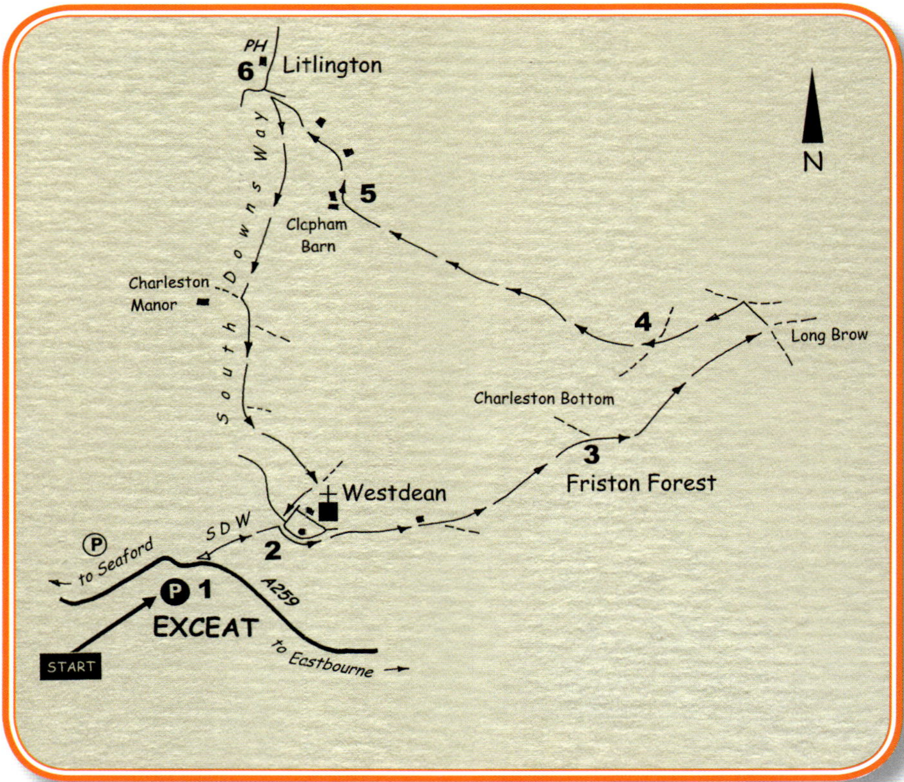

The Cuckmere valley at Exceat

The Walk

1 Walk back to the road and turn right to a bus stop before crossing to a **South Downs Way** fingerpost. Go ahead, pass through a kissing gate and continue on an uphill grassy path to a flint wall at the top of the slope. Cross the wall, turn right for a couple of yards before going left and following the path down steps to a quiet village road in **Westdean**.

2 Turn right here along **The Lane** and pass the ancient dovecote. When the road bends sharp left, go ahead on a track passing a **Friston Forest** sign. Press on along the unmade track and pass a vehicle barrier to meet a fork. Take the left fork and keep to the wide track. When a tarmac drive enters from the right, press on ahead and when it turns left, keep ahead to the crest of the rise.

3 Go through a gate, cross a meadow with extensive views and re-enter the woodland opposite. Follow the path until a wide crossing track is reached by a direction sign. Turn left and go downhill to a second crossing track and direction sign.

4 Ignore a wide crossing track here and press on ahead through trees to a gate at the edge of woodland. Pass through the gate and follow the left-hand field edge to another gate. Pass through this and now follow a cart track alongside fields with magnificent views towards the **White Horse** on **Hindover Hill** in the distance to reach **Clapham Barn**.

5 Follow the cart track to the right of the buildings and press on until a tarmac lane is met in **Litlington**. Our route turns left on the signed **South Downs Way** path, 50 yards before a T-junction. *(For refreshment at the Plough & Harrow pub, go ahead to the T-junction and turn right for 50 yards.)*

6 Turn left on the signed path that is also shared with the **Vanguard Way**. Climb a rise to the top left corner of a field before going ahead along the left side of the next field on the well-signed long-distance path. Now follow the long-distance path back to **Westdean** where you go ahead and retrace your earlier route by climbing the steps before descending through a field to rejoin the car park to end this great circuit.

What to look out for –

Medieval Dovecote

The route passes a well preserved 14th-century circular flint dovecote in Westdean. Although dovecotes can be of any shape, this circular free-standing design is typical of Sussex and inside are tiers of nesting ledges around the walls, with the roof topped by an open lantern from where the birds gained access. A ladder rotates around a central beam which enabled workers to harvest the eggs or the squabs for meat to supplement an often poor winter diet.

A dovecote of this size would generally house upwards of 450 birds and their droppings (guano) utilised as a fertiliser and also as an important source of saltpetre in the manufacture of gunpowder.

16 Burwash, Beak's Wood & Bateman's

Autumn

The route passes through a patchwork of scenic fields

This super route in the High Weald is wonderfully varied and good for any time of the year but is especially attractive when clothed in autumnal colours. Leaving Burwash behind on scenic field paths, the route crosses the River Dudwell before striking out across the vale for its furthest point on the heavily wooded slopes of Beak's Wood. The indigenous woodland is lovely at this time of year, with pocketfuls of ripe chestnuts just awaiting gathering. Heading back through Leggett's Wood on a charming woodland path, the route meets Park Farm before passing magnificent Bateman's house a short distance beyond. The way finally returns to Burwash on well-signed paths over peaceful pastures.

The Facts

Distance: 5½ miles

Terrain: Undulating, with one short noticeable hill.

Starting point: Public car park next to the Bear Inn, Burwash High Street (GR TQ674246).

How to get there: Burwash sits astride the A265, 7 miles east of Heathfield.

Map: OS Explorer 124 Hastings & Bexhill/Explorer 136 High Weald

Refreshments: The Bear Inn, Burwash, ☎ 01435 882540.

The Walk

1 With your back to the road, leave the car park on a signed path in its left corner. Follow the right side of an open space. Ignore a directional sign and press on to the bottom corner. Cross a stile and follow the path through woodland to a field. Turn right along the field edge and at the bottom corner go over a stile and footbridge before continuing along the left edge of a field to cross a stile and meet a lane.

2 Turn left along the lane to a road junction and turn right on the one signed to **Wood's Corner**. Cross the **River Dudwell** and soon turn left on a signed path at the entrance to **Riverdell Farm**. Pass the gates and press on ahead to cross a stile at a field edge. Go diagonally left to the corner of the field, enter the next field and continue along its left side. Cross a stile and go ahead up a slope to reach another field.

3 Now go right across the field and aim to the right edge of protruding woodland. Pass the woodland and press on to the far left corner of the field. Cross a stile, pass through a dell, forking right to enter a field. Go left along its edge until the hedgerow ends on your left. Here, fork right and pass between two oak trees to a footpath sign beside a paddock gate on the far side. Pass through the gate and continue along the left side of the paddock to reach a lane.

4 Turn right along the lane to the entrance to **Bonnet's Farm** and **Perryman's** on your left. Go left on a signed bridleway along their drive passing between

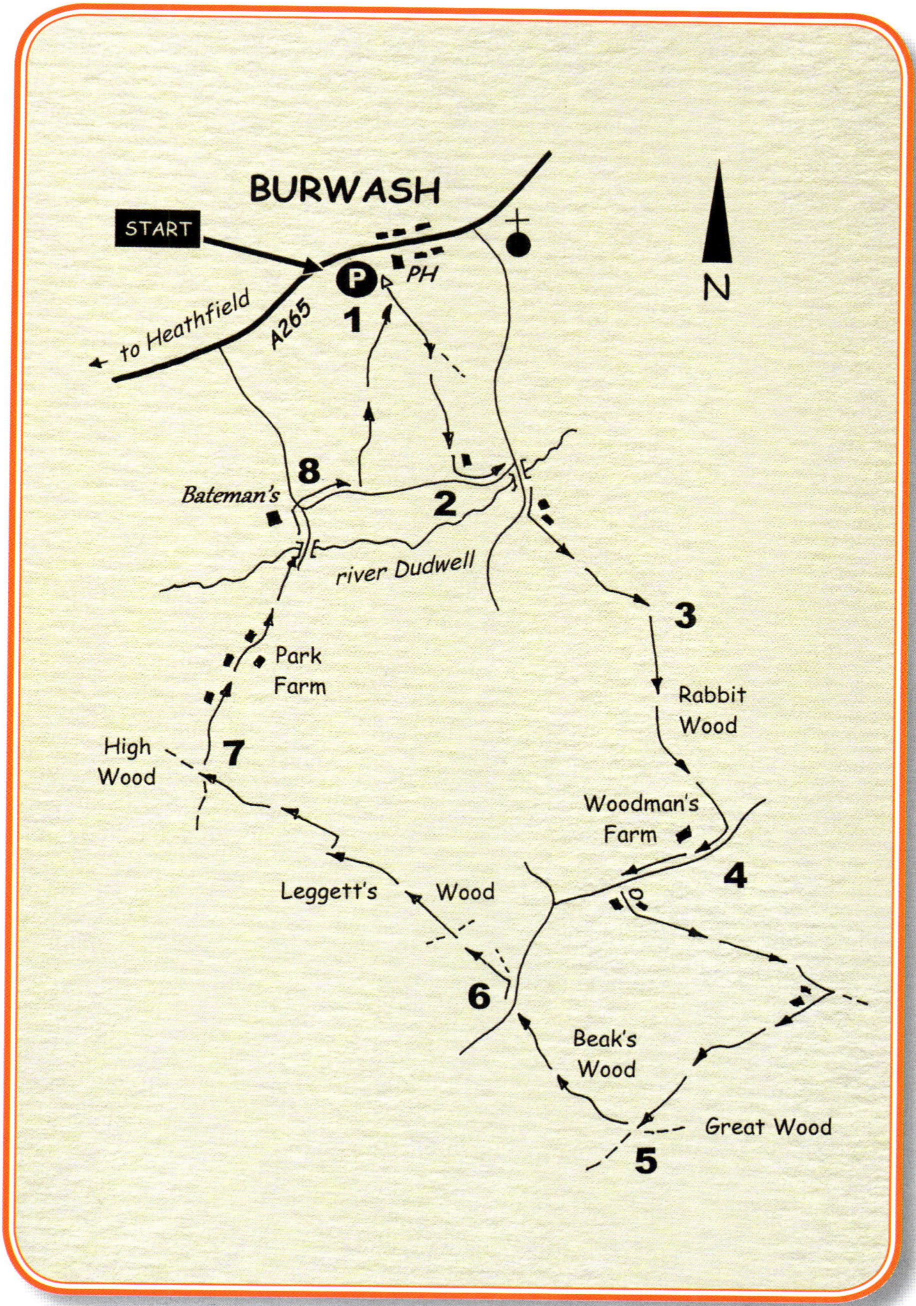
BURWASH
START
P
PH
to Heathfield
A265
N
1
2
3
4
5
6
7
8
Bateman's
river Dudwell
Park
Farm
High
Wood
Rabbit
Wood
Woodman's
Farm
Leggett's
Wood
Beak's
Wood
Great Wood

the house and a pond. At the end of a barn conversion, bear left on the grassy bridleway that later broadens and continues through woodland to meet a wooden building. Here ignore a drive leading to a house on your right but, 10 yards later, turn right on a signed bridleway that soon crosses a field and enters **Beak's Wood**.

The peaceful and tranquil High Weald

5 At the crest of a rise, pass under power cables and go down a dip to a bridleway sign and a path entering from the left. Turn right here on a narrow path between the trees and continue ahead after passing under power cables to reach the edge of the wood to enter a rising field. Press on along its left edge and at its top corner continue ahead to a road.

6 Turn right along the road and, in 140 yards, seek out a signed footpath on your left. Enter woodland and in 15 yards fork left on the signed path and keep ahead at crossing tracks. Later cross a footbridge before turning right as directed and soon bear left beside a gully before turning right over two further footbridges to a T-junction in 60 yards. Go left here to join a forestry track where the route continues ahead along it.

7 When the track reaches a clearing, go ahead to a directional post and turn right on the signed bridleway. At a field continue along its left edge and at its end go ahead along a ribbon of trees in a gully to meet the buildings of **Park Farm**. Press on along the farm drive passing the farmhouse and a cluster of houses. After crossing the **River Dudwell** the route reaches **Bateman's**.

8 Turn right along the lane opposite the house and, at a right bend, cross a stile in the hedgerow on your left and follow the right side of a field. Now press on along the well-signed path through fields to meet your outward route where a left turn brings you to the end of this good circuit.

Autumn

What to look out for –

Bateman's

As the route nears its end, it passes Bateman's, an attractive 17th-century Jacobean house believed to have been built by a local ironmaster. The house, watermill and surrounding 33 acres were purchased in 1902 by Rudyard Kipling for £9,300.

The famous novelist and poet had already written *The Jungle Book* and the *Just So Stories* by the time he came here but he produced many more works from this house including *Puck of Pook's Hill,* named after a hill visible from the house.

Kipling lived here until his death in 1936. The house was bequeathed to the National Trust as his memorial after his wife's demise three years later.

15 Historic Robertsbridge and its environs

Robertsbridge's historic High Street

This really good field path and farm drive circuit crosses attractive undulating Wealden countryside where the views are far-reaching. The walk starts by heading west on field paths to reach its first turning point at Squibs Farm. From here the way turns south and soon joins the scenic driveway of magnificent Hackwoods Farm before following a short section of country lane. Another wonderful farm drive leading to Bugsell and Beech Farms is followed before further field paths lead back to Robertsbridge. To complete the walk the way continues along the High Street where the fine 14th- and 15th-century Wealden Hall and timber-framed houses display the early prosperity of the village.

The Facts

Distance: 4¼ miles

Terrain: Undulating, with some mud after heavy rain.

Starting point: Car park beside a recreation ground off The Clappers (GR TQ740244).

How to get there: Robertsbridge is just west of the A21, 2 miles south of Hurst Green. The Clappers is a continuation of the High Street's northern end.

Map: OS Explorer 136 High Weald.

Refreshments: The Seven Stars pub, High Street, Robertsbridge, ☎ 01580 880333.

The Walk

1 From the car park, go back to the road and turn left beside it. At the end of the recreation ground, turn left and follow a fenced path alongside an old railway embankment before turning right under a bridge. In 10 yards turn left, pass through a gate and go ahead over an open area. Cross a footbridge and fork right to meet a boarded walkway before passing under a railway bridge.

2 In 20 yards turn right, cross a stile and follow a grassy path that soon bends left and continues up a slope to reach an open area. Fork right alongside a hedgerow and at a corner of the field, continue on a fenced path that skirts the field to cross a stile on your right.

3 Maintain your direction alongside a hedgerow and cross a stile in the corner. Continue ahead on a narrow path that leads to a large arable field. Cross the centre of the field and after going over a rise, bear slightly right and seek out a farm bridge in the hedgerow ahead.

4 Press on alongside a field and at a gap in the hedgerow ahead of you, continue along the left edge of the next field to reach **Squibs Farm**. With the farmhouse on your right and a barn to your left, turn left towards a wooden barn. Turn left before the barn on a signed path and continue downhill on the left side of a field. At a second field, press on ahead with a hedgerow on your right. Cross a concrete farm bridge and go ahead on a narrower uphill path.

Devotees of home-made sloe gin will find plentiful supplies of sloes along the route during autumn (see walk 12 for recipe).

The Wealden views are superb

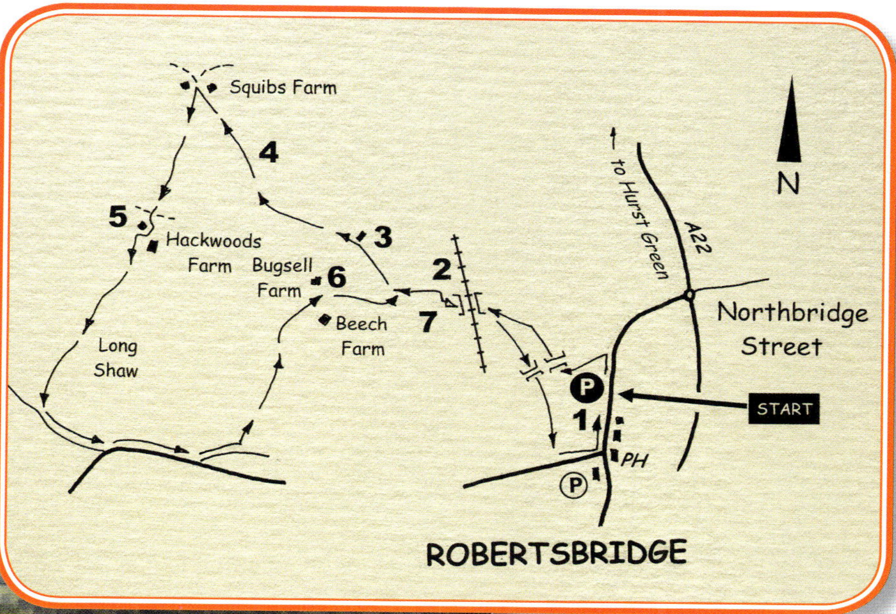

5 At the top of the rise, follow a path to the left of a house and pass its gateway to a drive. Continue along the drive passing the gate to **Hackwoods Farm** and remain on it until it ends at a lane. Turn left along the lane and at a road junction, turn left on the road signed to **Robertsbridge**. After passing well-appointed houses, turn left into **Bugsell Lane**. When the track divides, follow the left fork to pass **Bugsell Park** and reach the gateway to **Bugsell Farm**.

6 Cross a stile to the right of the gateway and continue on a well-trodden path skirting the grounds. Pass between fields, cross a stile and go ahead with a

hedgerow on your right. At the bottom of the slope, fork left to meet a tree-line and go left for 25 yards to rejoin your outward path which you should follow rightwards.

7 Remain on your outward route. Pass under the railway but leave your outward route when power cables are reached. Here turn right and follow their line to later pass under an old railway bridge. Follow the path through a meadow and later a small industrial site to reach **Station Road**. Turn left along the road to the historic **High Street** where a left turn returns you to the car park and the end of this good circuit.

What to look out for –

Medieval buildings

As the walk nears its end, it passes the Seven Stars pub, one of the earliest buildings in Robertsbridge and dating from 1400. Another building of the same year is Rosebank, further north along the High Street, while between them are numbers 25 and 27 that date from 1510. Tthe oldest surviving house is just off the High Street in Fair Lane and dates from 1390.

At the southern end of the High Street is an unusual clock tower war memorial built in 1928. More latterly, the village suffered severe flooding when in November 2000 the River Rother overflowed its banks damaging many properties and evidence of new flood defences will be seen near the car park.

16 Wilmington and the Long Man

The panorama from the lower slopes of Windover Hill

This spectacular walk around the South Downs above Wilmington is essentially one of two halves. Firstly, the route leaves the village via an old byway that brings you to the outskirts of Folkington village where a second, tree-lined byway with views of the rolling downs leads you to the route's furthest point. For the return, it follows the South Downs Way long-distance path across open downland where magnificent views stretch as far as the English Channel. After passing around the crest of Windover Hill, the path descends easily and passes the Long Man before finishing back at the village. This is a lovely winter walk and generally mud free so also good at any time of the year.

The Facts

Distance: 5¼ miles

Terrain: Hilly in parts but well within the capability of a person of average fitness.

Starting point: Car park by Wilmington Priory (GR TQ444042).

How to get there: Wilmington is signed off the A27, 2 miles west of Polgate. The car park is at the southern end of the village.

Map: OS Explorer 123 Eastbourne & Beachy Head.

Refreshments: The Giants Rest pub in Wilmington, ☎ 01323 870207

The Long Man of Wilmington

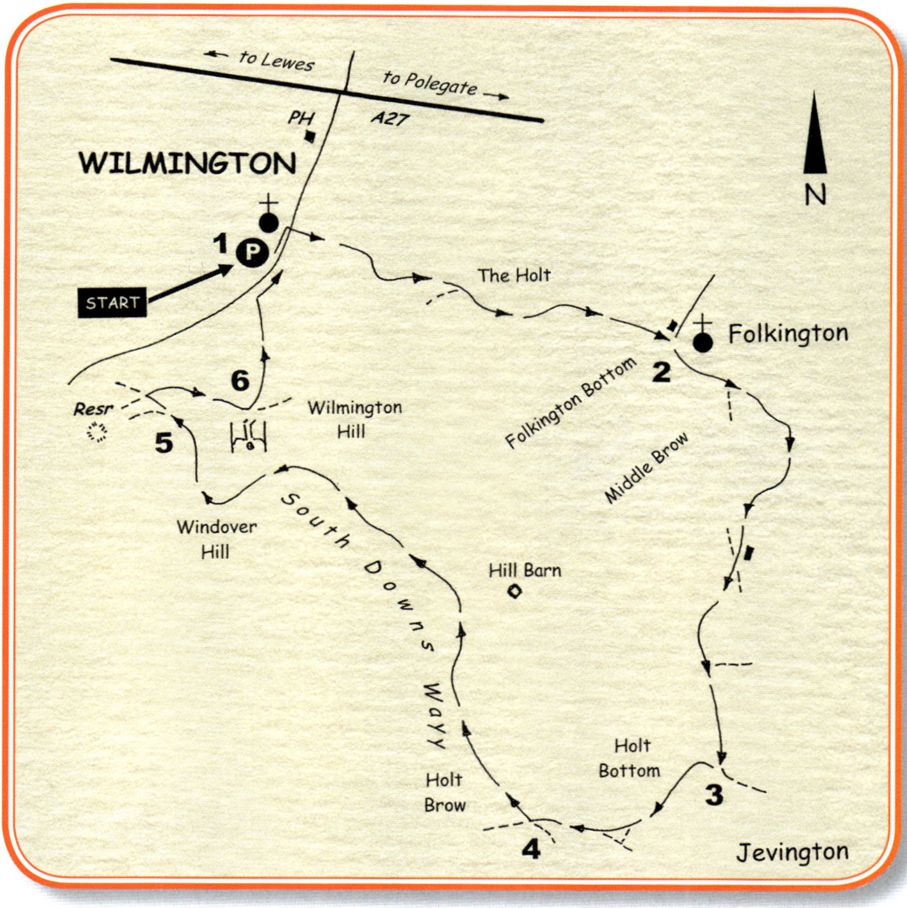

The Walk

1 From the car park entrance, turn left alongside the road to meet steps by the gate to the **church of St Mary and St Peter'**. Turn right here and continue along a stony byway that soon leaves the village behind. The byway climbs fairly easily and continues through lovely woodland alongside the escarpment of **The Holt**. After a gradual descent, the track brings you to a road by **St Peter's church** at **Folkington**.

2 Maintain your direction ahead along a wide byway that soon offers spectacular views of the rolling downs and remain on it until a T-junction is met after 1¼ miles.

3 Here, leave the byway by turning right on another wide bridleway. As it gains height, ignore a left fork and press on ahead to soon meet the **South Downs Way** path that joins from the left.

4 Continue ahead to reach a junction of tracks at the top of the incline. Turn right here on the signed **South Downs Way** to open grassland. Keep to the well-signed **South Downs Way** path as it passes through fields across the top of the downs and drink in the fantastic views it offers.

5 After rounding **Windover Hill**, the path descends and here you must make sure that when the track bends left, you do not miss a narrower path forking right beside a fence. After 100 yards, at a crossing path, turn right through a gate and follow the path to **The Long Man**.

6 Go left through a gate opposite the figure and continue towards the road and just before it, turn right on a fenced path that ends opposite the car park.

What to look out for –

The Long Man of Wilmington

It is unknown when the 235-ft-high Long Man, believed to be a Druid, was carved and by whom, although many Sussex people believe he was created by a monk from the nearby monastery.

A drawing by John Rowley in 1710 indicates that at that time it was only an indentation in the grass. By the late 1800s the outline was marked in yellow brick but during the Second World War the figure was painted green so as not to act as a landmark for enemy fliers.

In 1969 the bricks were replaced by concrete blocks that receive regular coats of white paint.

17 Forest Row and the High Weald Landscape Trail

Forest Way is a charming linear nature reserve

This peaceful rural walk well away from roads, leads you through lovely countryside within the High Weald Area of Outstanding Natural Beauty. Beginning near the centre of Forest Row, the way follows the High Weald Landscape Trail where, within minutes, the route passes through scenic fields and alongside indigenous woodland. After meeting the route's furthest point, it descends the ridge to meet up with Forest Way, once the track bed of a railway that has been transformed into a glorious linear country park that offers easy walking back to the village. Super as a winter walk because of the lack of mud and enjoyable year round.

The Facts

Distance: 5½ miles

Terrain: There is an easy rise of 220 ft over the first mile, after which it is either downhill or level.

Starting point: Car park beside the Community Centre in Hartfield Road (B2110) (GR TQ425350).

How to get there: From the mini roundabout on the A22 in the centre of the village, turn east along Hartfield Road (B2110) to meet the car park on your right in ¼ mile.

Map: OS Explorer 135 Ashdown Forest

Refreshments: Plenty of eateries in the village.

The Walk

1 Cross **Hartfield Road** to the small village green opposite. Bear left to reach **Station Road** and continue along it passing commercial buildings. Go ahead and left of the **Forest Lodge Veterinary Centre** to meet a track and turn rightwards along it. Ignore a **Forest Way** sign on your right and continue ahead on the track. Follow the track left at barns and when it soon turns right, press on ahead on the signed **High Weald Landscape Trail (HWLT)**.

2 At a gate, turn left on a well-trodden path, signed **HWLT,** to reach a squeeze stile. Go ahead and diagonally right and follow the field edge to its end to meet a cart track. Continue ahead here and when under power cables in woodland, ignore a path ahead and turn right on a well-trodden path to a T-junction.

3 Now go through a pedestrian gate. Ignore a path on your left and continue ahead on a well-trodden path that ends at a drive. Turn right along the drive passing **Blackberry Hill Farmhouse** and two other isolated houses to meet a left turn in the drive.

4 Leave the drive here. Ignore a bridleway ahead of you and cross a stile to its left and enter a field. Now follow an indistinct grassy path diagonally left to the far corner and press on to a marker post in 40 yards. Ignore a path signed leftwards and go ahead on the signed **HWLT**. Go downhill towards the left edge

of woodland from where you should bear left to a stile in the field corner.

5 Pass through lovely woodland to a field and continue ahead on the **HWLT** path as it follows the edge of fields. The route leaves the **HWLT** when a direction post is met opposite a barn behind the hedgerow.

6 Turn right here on a grassy path that leaves the ridge and soon skirts woodland before turning left along a field edge. Press on alongside a second field to reach the grounds of a remote house named **Lower Parrock**. Ignore a path on your left and continue ahead and rightwards around its perimeter to the driveway.

7 Turn left along the drive and cross the infant **River Medway** as you leave this idyllic spot to meet **Forest Way** by the driveway gates. Turn right now and follow this lovely linear nature reserve for 2 miles with views to either side.

The railway linked Three Bridges to Tunbridge Wells and although a successful commuter line, it was axed 100 years after its inception during the Beeching cuts. Having been bought in 1971 by East Sussex County Council, the disused line was named Forest Way and designated as a country park. More recently, Sustrans have included it in the National Cycle Network.

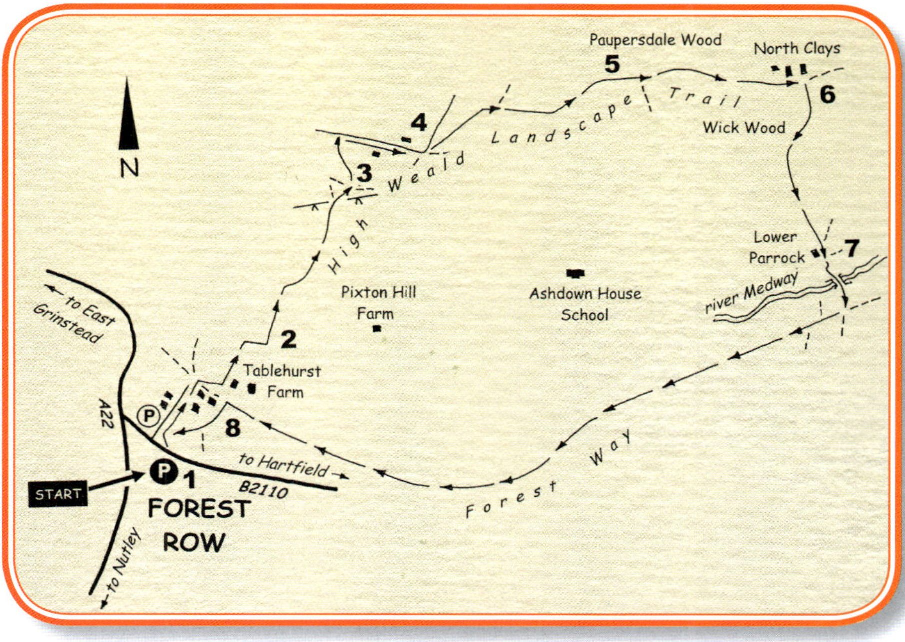

A sunken path near the start of the walk

8 Some 30 yards before an industrial building, turn left on a fenced path signed to **Forest Row Village** to rejoin the small village green with the car park and the end of the walk beyond.

What to look out for –

Hart's-tongue fern

Towards the end of the circuit, groups of hart's-tongue fern (*Phyllitis scolopendrium*) grow on the damp, shady banks of Forest Way. The plant, often sold commercially, is evergreen and unusual amongst ferns as it has simple, undivided fronds.

Its common name derives from the shape of the frond; hart being the old name for deer. The underside pictured here shows the pattern of spore capsules that are reminiscent of centipede legs from which its species name derives, *scolopendrium* – Latin for 'centipede'. The plant has been used in folk medicine as a tonic for the spleen while Culpeper, the 17th-century herbalist recommended it for *'the passions of the heart'*.

18

Firle Beacon & the South Downs Way

The summit of Firle Beacon

This spectacular downland walk has fabulous 360° views for its entire length and is an ideal circuit to stretch one's legs on a winter's day. The triangular route begins on top of the escarpment and passes easily over Firle Beacon, one of the highest points on the South Downs, before turning southwards towards the sea and gently descending over fields to reach the shelter of Stump Bottom. Beginning its return, the route follows a fold in the rolling downs before making its way up Blackcap Hill on a climb that should not trouble a person of average fitness. After passing Blackcap Farm the way soon rejoins the top of the downs to complete this excellent walk.

The Facts

Distance: 5½ miles

Terrain: Undulating, with one steady rise of 270 ft. Good for any time of the year although some mud may be encountered during winter.

Starting point: Firle Beacon car park (GR TQ468059).

How to get there: From the A27, 3½ miles east of Lewes, turn south on a road signed to Firle. Soon fork right on a lane signed to Firle Beacon and follow it to the car park on top of the downs.

Map: OS Explorer 123 Eastbourne & Beachy Head

Refreshments: The Ram Inn, Firle, ☎ 01273 858222

Winter

The Walk

1 With your back to the lane, pass through a pedestrian gate near the left end of the car park and go ahead on the signed **South Downs Way** path. Follow the wide indistinct grassy path for 1 mile along the top of the downs and cross the summit of **Firle Beacon** that is marked by a trig point.

At 217 metres high, Firle Beacon qualifies as a Marilyn. The name is a pun contrasting with that of the Scottish Munroes that are much higher, of course. From this vantage point there is a good chance of spotting buzzards soaring on the thermals created by the escarpment.

2 Press on ahead and in ½ mile look out for a post on your left and a gate opposite on your right, both marked with blue arrows (bridleway sign). Leave the long-distance path now by turning right through the gate and follow the bridleway over a sloping field towards a gate ½ mile ahead of you.

3 Maintain your direction towards the sea on the marked bridleway as it crosses **Heighton Hill**. Later it narrows and continues along a field edge as it descends to meet **Stump Bottom** in the valley below.

4 Turn right here on a signed bridleway that follows the valley floor and brings you to the foot of **Blackcap Hill**. Press on ahead along the bridleway that begins to rise quite sharply as it heads for a line of trees on the skyline.

5 Walk on through the tree line and soon the climb eases. Continue between the buildings of **Blackcap Farm** and follow the farm drive back to the car park to end this scenic route.

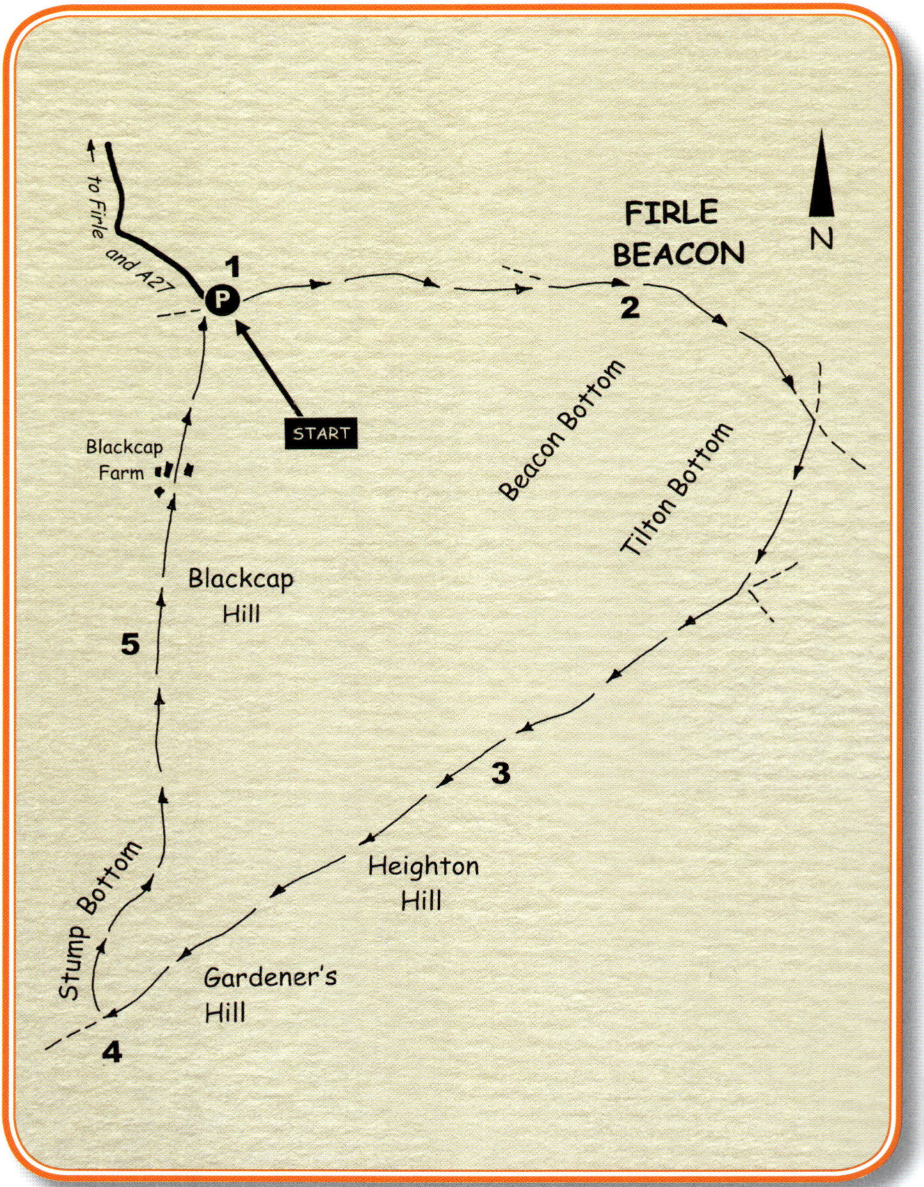

Hardy residents of Firle Beacon

What to look out for –

Lichen

The barn roof of Blackcap Farm will be seen glowing gold in the sun across the vale on your right at point 3 of the circuit. This remarkable colouring is due to a very large colony of the lichen *(Caloplaca flavesens)*.

Lichen is an association between fungi and algae; neither able to live in isolation. These two unlike organisms survive by symbiosis. The algae produce carbohydrates from the air and water via photosynthesis while the fungi, which are the dominant partner, are a welcome parasite.

Almost all lichen are asexual, which means they are both male and female and when their spores are released on the breeze, each will need to find its correct algal partner for it to germinate.

Winter

19 The fields of Fletching and Piltdown

The circuit begins in Fletching's main street

This really good field walk leaves Fletching by going southwards over fields with panoramic views on well-signed paths to reach the hamlet of Piltdown, a name forever associated with one of the world's greatest archeological hoaxes. Swinging east over the manicured grasses of Piltdown golf course, the route soon turns once again and heads for Mallingdown Farm from where the final leg begins as further scenic field paths lead the way towards the spire of Fletching's church to complete this enjoyable circuit. A good walk for any time of the year and due to the lack of mud is ideal during winter.

Distance: 4 miles

Terrain: Lightly undulating.

Starting point: Car park off Fletching High Street (GR TQ429235).

How to get there: From the A272 at Piltdown, turn north on Ruston Bridge Road to meet Fletching in 1 mile. The car park is opposite the Griffin Inn.

Map: OS Explorer 135 Ashdown Forest

Refreshments: The Griffin Inn, ☎ 01825 722890.

The Walk

1 When facing the **Griffin Inn**, turn left and soon pass through the gate of **Fletching's** churchyard. Continue around the front of the church to its main door and turn right to rejoin the road. Cross the road. Turn left and at the pavement end, go through a gate ahead to enter a recreation ground. Proceed ahead to the corner then turn right along its boundary and exit via a metal stile. Follow a path under power cables until you reach a signed path on your left.

2 Turn left here and cross large fields on a well-defined path. Be aware that at the end of the second field the path crosses a grass landing strip. Press on to the left of a small hangar and continue along a drive to the A272. Turn left alongside the road for 20 yards before crossing to ornate gates and over a stile to their right. Continue on a fenced path to cross another stile.

3 Turn left here over a wooden bridge and continue on a fenced path alongside paddocks until it ends at a cart track. Turn right to soon reach a driveway which you should follow and later pass the gates to **Barkham Manor**.

Barkham Manor became entangled in one of history's greatest hoaxes when skull fragments were discovered here in a gravel pit in 1912. Neanderthals had already been discovered in Europe but this find, later know as Piltdown Man, was thought to provide proof of the 'missing link' between ape and man. It took 40 years for the truth to come out. The skull was indeed human but only 500 years old, while the jaw came from an orang-utan.

The path leaving Piltdown

4 When the drive ends at a lane, go ahead on a signed footpath that leads across a golf course. Maintain direction aiming to the left of a house in the trees ahead to meet a road. Turn right alongside the road for 25 yards before going left on a signed path to rejoin the golf course.

5 At a low marker post in 40 yards, turn left to reach a second low marker post in 35 yards. Turn right here and pass the 4th tee to reach another post beside trees. Go ahead on a broad path and look out for a post on your right in 20 yards. Turn right and pass a green to reach a seat and another post. Now go ahead between trees and continue on a path over an unruly part of the course to the left of a green. Enter woodland, cross a brick bridge and continue alongside the grounds of a house. Keep to the well-signed path through woodland to reach a private drive.

❻ Turn right along the drive and 50 yards before its end, fork left to meet the A272. Turn right alongside the road for 30 yards before crossing to the drive of **Little Ferrars**. Go up the drive and in 15 yards turn right over a stile. Go ahead and pass to the right of a woodland pond and cross a second stile to enter a small paddock. Continue ahead and pass through a gate to the drive of **Oak Ferrars Farm**.

❼ Go ahead on an indistinct path with industrial units to your left. The path soon broadens and continues alongside woodland with fields to your left. The path ends at the driveway of **Mallingdown Farm**. Turn left along the farm drive and soon pass the front of the farmhouse and **Mallingdown Oast** soon after.

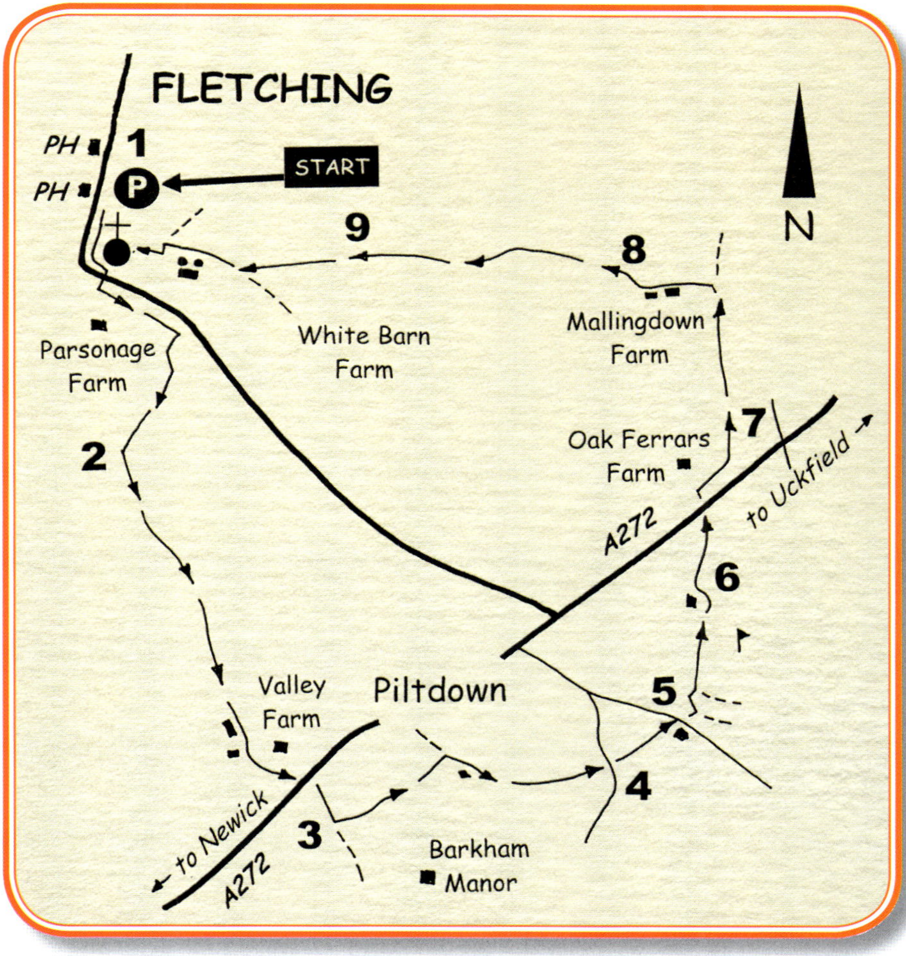

8 Continue ahead on the well-signed path. Later pass through a squeeze stile and continue between hedgerows before pressing on along a field edge. Cross a stile at the field end and turn right along the next field edge and cross a stile in the hedgerow on your right. Turn left and cross a stile in the hedgerow ahead to enter a large field. Maintain direction and cross a metal stile on the brow of a low rise.

9 Press on ahead aiming to the left of the church steeple. Go over a stile in the hedgerow ahead and turn right along a cart track which soon bends left. Here go over a metal stile on your right and continue along a field edge before passing to the right of a barn and silos to meet a kissing gate and enter a churchyard. Turn left along the boundary before going right on a grassy path and passing the side of the church to reach **Fletching's High Street** where a right turn brings you to the car park.

What to look out for –

Fletching church memorials

St Andrew & St Mary the Virgin church contains interesting memorials; the earliest dates from 1380 and depicts Sir Walter Dalyngrigge and his wife, whose son went on to build Bodiam Castle.

The brass shows Sir Walter in full armour of the period while his wife lies beside him dressed in a cloak and gown. The memorial once had a stone canopy but that was lost to decay in 1820.

Hard to miss is the outstanding, life-size alabaster effigies of Richard Leche, High Sheriff of Sussex and Surrey, and his wife Charitie. Leche died in 1596 and although his wife later remarried, she instructed that on her death she was to be interred with her first husband.

20 Mayfield and Coggins Mill

The route offers lovely views

This superb winter walk leads you through a patchwork of scenic fields in this area of the High Weald to the south and east of Mayfield village. By utilizing a combination of grassy field paths, quiet lanes and charming farm drives, the route avoids most of the winter's mud. After leaving Mayfield, the way first crosses a small valley before heading east along ancient sunken tracks towards Merrieweathers and Sharnden Old Manor farms. Reaching the quiet hamlet of Coggins Mill, the route continues through peaceful Vicarage Wood before crossing more scenic fields on its return, where a short stroll along Mayfield's historic High Street completes the circuit. This is a lovely walk for any time of the year.

Distance: 4¼ miles

Terrain: Undulating

Starting point: Mayfield village car park (GR TQ588268).

How to get there: Mayfield is signed off the A267, 5 miles north of Heathfield. The car park is signed from the centre of the High Street.

Map: OS Explorer 136 High Weald

Refreshments: The Middle House Hotel, High Street, Mayfield, ☎ 01435 872146

The Walk

1 With your back to the car park, turn right along the narrow lane. Press on until just before a T-junction, turn right on a signed path beside a house named **Flower Place**. Enter a field and continue on the well-signed path along the right

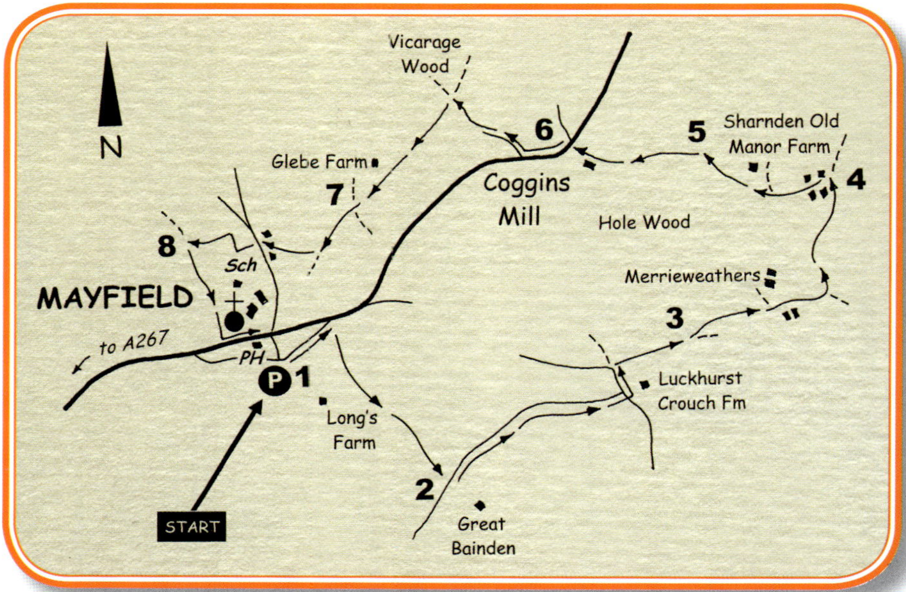

Crossing a woodland brook

side of four fields. Cross a bridge in a woodland dell and continue ahead on the path to reach a lane.

2 Go left along the lane and when it ends at a T-junction, turn left on the road signed to **Mayfield**. The route soon leaves the road at a left bend 20 yards before the gates of **Five Gables**. Ignore a path to the right of the gates and turn sharp right on a bridleway along a track signed to **Stonycroft**. Press on along this lovely track between ancient banks to reach a fork.

3 Keep left at the fork and continue along the sunken bridleway. Ignore a footpath on your left at buildings and remain on the bridleway that passes the grounds of **Merrieweathers**. Keep left at a fork; cross a woodland stream and continue alongside the grounds and ignore a path to your right.

4 At dilapidated barns, follow the bridleway left between buildings and continue up a rise. Leave the bridleway here when it turns right and continue ahead. Ignore two paths on your left, cross a stile ahead and press on along the right-hand field edge. Cross a woodland stream and go ahead for 45 yards to a low marker post.

5 Turn left here with a hedgerow on your right and continue along the field edge. Towards the field end, bear left on the grassy path to cross a stile. Pass a barn and press on along the path; pass a house and continue along its drive to a road.

6 Turn left along the road and in the hamlet of **Coggins Mill**, turn right along a small lane with a footpath signed to **Little Trogers Lane**. At the lane end, continue ahead through **Vicarage Wood** to a directional post and a crossing path. Turn left here. Go up a rise and after leaving woodland, press on alongside three fields.

7 At the end of the third field, ignore side paths and keep ahead to a cart track. Turn right along the track and pass between houses to a road. Cross the road and continue up the drive to **St Leonard's-Mayfield School** to meet a marker post on a bend. Turn right here. Continue alongside an all-weather pitch and at its end, turn left beside them on the signed path that later passes a pond and ends at a T-junction.

8 Turn left at this T-junction and continue alongside the school grounds before forking left at a rough parking area. Pass between a cemetery and allotments and finally cottages to reach **Mayfield High Street**. Turn left and pass **The Middle House** before turning right to the car park and the end of this good circuit.

What to look out for –

The Middle House

Mayfield enjoyed a boom time at the height of the Wealden iron industry and its High Street contains some of the oldest and best architecture in East Sussex from those days. Prosperous families lived in the fine houses that line the High Street which is well worth investigating, with one outstanding building in particular – 16th-century Middle House, now a hotel.

This impressive Elizabethan timber-framed, three-storey building was once owned by Sir Thomas Gresham, keeper of the Privy Purse for Elizabeth l. The house remained as a private residence up until the 1920s and contains a splendid Grinling Gibbons carved fireplace, wattle and daub walls and a private chapel.